Microwave Game & Fish Cookbook

Microwave Game & Fish Cookbook

Quick, convenient recipes for concocting
the tastiest, juiciest, most succulent
wild meat and fish meals you've ever eaten

Paula J. Del Giudice

Stackpole Books

Copyright © 1985 by Stackpole Books

Published by
STACKPOLE BOOKS
Cameron and Kelker Streets
P.O. Box 1831
Harrisburg, PA 17105

All rights reserved, including the right to reproduce this book or portions thereof in any form or by any means, electronic or mechanical, including photocopying, recording, or by any information storage and retrieval system, without permission in writing from the publisher. All inquiries should be addressed to Stackpole Books, Cameron and Kelker Streets, P.O. Box 1831, Harrisburg, Pennsylvania 17105.

Printed in the U.S.A.

Library of Congress Cataloging in Publication Data

Del Giudice, Paula J.
   Microwave game & fish cookbook.

    Includes index.
    1. Microwave cookery. 2. Cookery (Game) 3. Cookery (Fish) I. Title. II. Title: Microwave game and fish cookbook.
TX832.D45   1984   641.6'91   84-24000
ISBN 0-8117-2191-4

To my father, Paul J. Del Giudice, M.D.
He has always given so much to everyone
and asked so little in return.

Contents

Foreword   9

Acknowledgments   11

A Feast in Minutes   13

Upland Game Birds   17

   Chukar
   Dove
   Grouse
   Pheasant
   Quail
   Woodcock and Jacksnipe

Waterfowl   44

   Duck
   Goose

Small Game   57
Rabbit
Squirrel

Mixed Bag   68
Ground Hog
Raccoon
Wild Boar

Big Game   74
Antelope
Deer
Elk
Moose and Caribou

Fresh Water Catch   103
Bass
Catfish
Panfish
Salmon
Trout
Walleye and Pike

Fish from the Deep   138
Flounder
Halibut
Sturgeon

Appetizers   146

Serve Alongs   155

Sauces, Butters, and Marinades   170

Convert Your Own Recipes   180

Defrosting Guide   184

Index   187

Foreword

When Paula Del Giudice asked me to write the foreword for this book, I'll admit I was a bit skeptical. I do a fair amount of wild game cooking, but never in my microwave. The device has always been viewed with suspicion when it came to outright *cooking* and was basically used to warm cold coffee and leftovers. Furthermore, wild game tends to be dry, which was another reason I distrusted the microwave.

I told Paula my apprehensions, and she immediately fired off an antelope recipe, but not without a substantial amount of good-natured warning.

"You're going to love it," she said.

"I doubt it," I responded, "but if I do, I'll write the foreword for your book."

I cooked the antelope in my microwave, I loved it, so now I'm writing the foreword.

With the antelope repast a delightful memory, I asked Paula for more recipes. She obliged, and I'm a believer. No longer will my microwave be relegated to mundane chores. It's a major appliance in the kitchen now, and, thanks to Paula, I've added a new dimension to my wild game cooking.

Microwave cooking makes sense in our hectic society. It's quick, it's easy, and it turns out gourmet feasts that must be tasted to be believed.

Paula's talents don't rest merely in the kitchen. I've known her since she was senior editor of a shooting/hunting magazine, and she's an avid hunter and angler who brings home fish and game more often than not.

Oh—don't challenge her at the trapshooting range, lest you can stand to be soundly trounced.

A word of warning as you read this book and begin experimenting with your microwave. Don't be surprised if you find yourself trekking the woods, prairies, and streambanks with more vigor and enthusiasm than normal. You'll savor wild critters more than ever before, and you'll be grateful for Paula's hard work in her kitchen to produce and test these superb recipes.

But don't take my word for it. Try some yourself—but make sure you have plenty for second helpings. I guarantee there'll be a demand for them at your dinner table.

Jim Zumbo, Editor-at-large
Outdoor Life

Acknowledgments

No book ever published is a true solitary effort. There are many people who were responsible for this cookbook and, while these few written words couldn't possibly convey my heartfelt appreciation, I'd like to thank them.

Paul J. Del Giudice, M.D.—my father—for his patience and support during the lonely hours I spent researching, testing recipes, and writing this book.

Paul J. Del Giudice, Jr. and Dick Del Giudice—two of my brothers—for their love and encouragement.

My aunts and my uncle—Rose, Nettie, Jane, and Uncle Joe—for always helping out with everything.

Tom and Dorothy Gallagher for their support, recipes, and for filling in the spaces in my freezer with game when I needed it.

Judy Hicks—my best friend—and her husband, Larry, for always being there with a shoulder when I have questioned my sanity.

Judith M. Schnell—my editor at Stackpole—who made the process of completing my first book a somewhat painless experience.

Jim Zumbo—the author of the foreword—for advice and help he gave me with this project.

My friends, especially Kathy Alley and Kristin Colongeli, my peers, my editors, and the rest of my family for their understanding and moral support.

Ruth Roseberry of Elko, Nevada—my grammar school English teacher—for teaching me the structure of the English language, enabling me to create for myself a rewarding career.

A Feast in Minutes

    I learned to use the microwave oven out of self-defense. The busier I became with my writing career, the less time I had for cooking meals. Now don't get me wrong. I love to cook. I've been cooking for my family as long as I've been able to reach the stove. Even before that, I practiced on the top of an old radiator just the right height for a young girl's cooking fancies.

    About eighty-five percent of my family's diet consists of wild game and fish. Whatever happens to be in season is the specialty of the house. We enjoy the outdoors so much and enjoy harvesting game and catching fish. We are strong believers in taking good care of our bounty so that none of our hard-earned meat is spoiled. I feel privileged to be able to take advantage of our outdoor resources and I strive to remain within the legal and ethical boundaries set for outdoorsmen.

    Enjoying a meal with game meat, birds, or fish as the main course is such an honor that it fills me with an enormous amount of pride. Sharing a meal of this sort with my friends and loved ones is especially pleasurable.

After stalking and killing my game cleanly, field dressing with care for the meat, aging and cutting the meat, and cooking it to perfection, I have thoroughly tested and honed my skills as an outdoorsman. The meal that follows is the reward.

The microwave oven now found in many households is the working cook's benefactor. Since it cooks so many things so quickly and easily it is a natural for wild fish and game. The more I used my microwave for whole meal cooking, the more I began to search for recipes for wild game or fish that could be used in the microwave. Since I couldn't find very many, I invented my own or converted my favorite recipes to suit whatever it was I was preparing. Basically, that is how this cookbook evolved.

Some outdoorsmen are bound to consider cooking fish or game in the microwave an abomination. It's not my absolute favorite way of cooking game either, but it's an excellent alternative. I think there's nothing better than the smell of venison stew simmering on the back burner for hours while the yeast bread is rising in a warm spot. If I had my druthers, I'd cook over coals. Many times I don't have the time to make those preparations and the microwave cooks my meal in about a quarter of the time.

I can't advocate selling your conventional oven or your smoker or your stove top or your crockpot. Each of these more traditional means of preparing your meat or fish has its place in your kitchen's repertoire. But microwaving is a wonderful method for cooking food and an excellent addition to any game cook's kitchen. I'm especially grateful for my microwave oven when the temperature is soaring outside and my kitchen's bordering on a heat wave. The microwave won't greet you with a blast of hot air when you open the door.

There are two favorite techniques for cooking game recommended by top game cooks. One is to cook hot and fast. The other is to slow cook. The slow cooking method usually employs the wet cooking idea of simmering game in some sort of liquid until it is thoroughly cooked, absorbing as much of the liquid as possible to keep the meat moist. The microwave is excellent for this type of cooking. The only difference is that it cooks the meat in a much shorter period of time. There is a disadvantage to that. For instance, when you cook a hearty stew the slow cooking allows all the flavors to meld. I've found that cooking the stews and soups ahead of the time they're needed and refrigerating them overnight solves this problem. Then the microwave is a snap for warming them up again.

Most cooks who have little success in cooking fish or seafood have two problems. Either the fish they've chosen to cook is too old from sitting in the freezer or the refrigerator too long, or the fish is overcooked. The first problem must be solved by the cook and is easily corrected. Only cook the freshest of fish and, if you must freeze the fish, make sure to cook it as soon as possible. Cooking fish in the microwave is a delightful solution to the overcooking problem. In a few short minutes, the microwave cooks your fish gently. Because the microwave is not a source of direct heat, the natural moisture of the fish is not baked away.

I was a little intimidated by the microwave oven at first because I really didn't understand how to use it to its best advantage. I used it for pretty much the same purposes as you do: defrosting, warming bread, cooking hot dogs, melting cheese, melting butter. Before too long, I was using the microwave almost exclusively.

I was also intimidated by what I'd read about the microwave, especially regarding roasting large cuts of meat or whole birds. At first I was a little apprehensive about cooking a marvelous goose in the oven, for instance, until I tried it. The results were excellent. Of course, the microwave doesn't brown like a conventional oven, but I don't find that a drawback. If you really want something browned, place it under the broiler in your conventional oven for a few moments and that problem is solved.

Of course, the microwave reacts like a conventional oven when cooking meat that is lean so you should be very careful not to overcook it. A temperature probe or meat thermometer solves this problem easily. I think you'll like the results on whole ducks, geese, leg of wild boar, fish, and game birds.

In this cookbook, I've tried to avert any surprises. You should be able to use this cookbook with ease, confident that your recipes will meet your expectations. I've tried to convey to you any tips I've picked up along the way.

This cookbook is not meant to be used in place of a general cookbook on microwave cooking. I'm assuming you own one of those already. I've excluded the sections on the theory of microwave cooking. There are no discussions on the proper types of microwave cookware. If you are unfamiliar with general microwave cooking, you may want to brush up on the information available before using a recipe from this cookbook.

I've tried to be as generic as possible when recommending the proper cooking utensils for these recipes. I've tried to keep my recommendations as simple as possible and I've employed as many familiar household cookware items as I could, so you won't need to purchase special equipment.

Our family is very conscientious about our eating habits. We try to hold the line on fatty meat and we try to keep our intake of salt and sugar down. Game meat and fish are excellent alternatives to the fat problem since their fat content is much lower than that of the highly marbled beef bred for consumption. In most of the recipes in this book, I've cut down or cut out the salt listed in the ingredients. Many of the recipes state "to taste." I'd recommend using the salt sparingly. It's up to you whether or not you'll want to add salt to your meals.

Because our family's just like yours when it comes to watching our weight, I try to contain many fresh vegetables and fruits in my menus. I hope you'll enjoy the recipes where I've included them. The cooking times I've suggested for sautéing vegetables in the microwave may provide a vegetable that seems undercooked to you. I prefer vegetables that are firm and crunchy instead of wet, overcooked, and soggy. If this new texture is unfamiliar or undesirable to you, cook the veggies just a little bit longer.

I've tried to include a wide variety of dishes in this cookbook. Also, I've included items you'd think would be impossible to cook in the microwave just to show you how versatile the microwave oven is. You'll find dishes to whip up on a minute's notice that will please even the pickiest eaters.

Don't hesitate to change any of the particular seasonings I've used or adjust them to suit your own particular tastes. I like to combine seasonings that are well-suited to each other and the dish they're complementing. If I've included more garlic than you're inclined to use, please don't hesitate to cut down on the amount you use. I'm Italian and I love garlic. Most people don't have taste buds that will accommodate as much garlic as I use. I grow many of my own herbs and vegetables such as garlic (of course), basil, and savory, because I like the taste of fresh herbs better than dried ones.

One ingredient I recommend you don't scrimp on is butter. Although butter is more expensive than margarine, the flavor is worth the price. The caloric value is the same, so if you're counting calories and the recipe is loaded with margarine or butter, you've already blown it.

With the microwave, any variation in the size of the cooking dish, a variation in the amount of liquid involved, the humidity in the air, will all affect your cooking times. The best recommendation I can make: when cooking any fish or game in the microwave, don't overcook it. Cook the dish at the lowest recommended time, then increase the time if necessary. Allow for the cooking to finish once the dish is removed from the oven. The best way to ruin your meat is to overcook it. Most game is best if the juices are still running a little pink, except for rabbit which should be cooked more thoroughly. Usually the sitting time will finish the dish to perfection.

I hope you'll enjoy the other recipes I've included to serve as side dishes with fish or wild game. Most of them require at least the partial use of the microwave. I've included some of our family favorites as well as more traditional fixings.

I must take this opportunity to thank my recipe taste-tester, my father Paul J. Del Giudice. He was instrumental in developing this cookbook. He indulged in the successful dishes. Thanks go to our golden retriever Dolly who gormandized on the unsuccessful ones. Well, okay, she got some of the good ones, too.

Eating is a celebration. Cooking should not be a hindrance to the event. Wild game and freshly caught fish are best when cooked very simply. When you're planning menus, keep the color of the food in mind. The visual aspect of your meal is as important as the taste. Your table setting is equally important visually. When the meal is served, savor the taste of the food you've prepared. The taste of every bird, animal, or fish is different. Just as pork tastes different than beef, antelope has a different flavor than elk. If the game is well taken care of, you won't need a strong sauce to mask the flavor of the meat. I've tried to keep the sauces from overpowering the delicate flavor of your game or fish.

I hope you'll enjoy trying these recipes as much as I enjoyed developing them for you.

Upland Game Birds

Chukar

Chukars might as well be dubbed the regional bird of the West. Nearly every western state has huntable populations of chukars. The top chukar producers have typically been Washington, Oregon, Idaho, and Nevada.

Since I was born in one of the most popular areas for hunting chukars anywhere in the West—Elko, Nevada—I became a fan of the wily critter at an early age.

In fact the first game bird I ever ate was a chukar. I found out early that no matter which method you use to cook birds, if you overcook them you're out of luck. The first time I ate chukar, it was badly overcooked. It tasted something like I'd expect boot leather to taste if I were ever inclined to eat boot leather. I couldn't imagine what all the fuss was about. It didn't seem like much fun to get up very, very early in the morning and walk all day long for a few birds that were dry and tasteless.

It's a shame to ruin good game meat, especially since it's so easy to do that in the microwave. But chukars can be done superbly in the microwave, very quickly. I'm not in favor of wasting any game meat, and it seems an extreme shame especially when you've gone through so much trouble to get them. Chukar hunting in the West is for the stouthearted since the birds live in some of the godawfullest places—high on rocky ledges, in steep canyons. Look at the worst countryside you can find in the West and if there's water and cheatgrass nearby, chances are there'll be some chukars there, too.

Hunting chukars in the West has a sort of mystique to it. I would venture a guess that the chukar is the most popular of all western game birds. As such, the chukar hunt is becoming a tradition in the West. While southerners gather for the annual dove hunt complete with trimmings, westerners have surrounded their annual chukar hunts with similar traditions, albeit not as grandiose.

No game cookbook would be complete without some favorite chukar recipes. Since this cookbook was conceived right smack in the heart of terrific chukar hunting country, I would be remiss not to mention a few recipes.

No extraordinary care need be taken with the birds after they're shot, but it helps to pull the crop out of the birds if you're not going to clean them thoroughly at the time they're shot. This helps keep the birds tasting their best.

If you're still eating chukars out of your freezer right before the season is due to open again, you're probably freezer burning your birds. You should plan to eat the birds, ideally, before six months are up.

Chukar meat tends to be a little bit drier than other game birds, I've found. It helps to undercook them just a shade and then allow them to finish cooking outside the microwave. If you cover them with foil for at least five minutes before serving, they'll come out just right.

Sweet sauces complement the flavor of the chukar, so even if it tends to be a little dry, a sauce may help. If you happen to get into some birds that are a little dry, cover them with foil and while they're finishing their cooking, whip up your favorite warm sauce to serve over them. The currant sauce in this book tastes great with chukars, but if you don't have any of those ingredients, mix some jelly or jam (peach, apricot, apple, pineapple, or marmalade) with a few teaspoons of wine or vinegar to cut the sweetness and impart a little tartness. This tip might save your dinner. No one will ever know that your birds were a little dry. In fact, many game cooks mix up the sauce as a matter of course.

GRILLED CHUKAR
Serves 4

4 chukars
½ cup barbecue sauce

Place chukars in a baking dish just large enough to hold them. Brush with barbecue sauce. Cover.

Microwave the chukars on 80 percent setting for 4 minutes on one side, turn. Microwave 4 minutes more.

Finish cooking on a grill over hot coals until juice of the chukars runs clear.

Note: What's a barbecue recipe doing in a microwave cookbook? The microwave is a good way to give a boost to the cooking time of a barbecue. The sauce won't burn and neither will the delicate birds if done this way.

DR. TOM'S 40 GARLIC CHUKAR

Serves 4

4 *chukars*
½ *onion, cut in half lengthwise and separated into sections*
1 *teaspoon dried parsley*
1 *teaspoon thyme*
4 *bay leaves, whole, plus 1 bay leaf, crumbled*
⅔ *cup olive oil*
1 *teaspoon ground sage*
1 *teaspoon rosemary, crumbled*
1 *teaspoon dried thyme*
   Salt and pepper
40 *unpeeled garlic cloves (about 4 large heads of garlic)*
3 *tablespoons water*

Separate the onion sections. Keep the four smallest one. In each of four sections, sprinkle ¼ teaspoon parsley, ¼ teaspoon thyme, and 1 whole bay leaf. Set aside.

In a heavy stovetop skillet, heat olive oil. Add crumbled bay leaf, sage, rosemary, and dried thyme to oil. Add chukars. Brown chukars on all sides in oil. Remove from oil and dust with salt and pepper.

Stuff an onion section into each body cavity. Tie legs together with string to hold onion in place. Place small pieces of aluminum foil around ends of legs to keep legs from overcooking. Make sure pieces of foil do not touch each other and are at least 1 inch from oven walls. Place birds in an 8-inch square glass dish. Add garlic cloves around birds. Add water to bottom of dish.

Cover tightly. Microwave on 60 percent or bake for 18–19 minutes. Remove from the oven. Cover with aluminum foil, shiny side down, for at least 5 minutes before serving.

Note: Dr. Tom Gallagher was my childhood dentist and longtime family friend. He can't stand garlic, but he has had to tolerate its notorious odor for many, many years as an innocent bystander—a hazard of his profession. He is also an avid shotgunner and hunter. I raided his freezer to test some of the recipes for this cookbook, including this one for 40 Garlic Chukar.

Just for you, Tom, the garlic won't be missed too much if you leave it out of this recipe.

Traditionally, the garlic cloves are served with the birds. The creamy cooked cloves are pressed out and spread on pieces of toast. In the traditional recipe, chicken is cooked instead of chukars. But the spices in the recipe work great with the chukars.

In a regular oven, the cloves become browned. This won't happen in the microwave, but for those who like garlic, serve it with pieces of toast anyway. The cooked cloves taste completely different than you would imagine.

CHUKAR AU VIN
Serves 4

    4 *chukars, cut into serving pieces*
       Flour for dredging
½ *cup butter*
 1 *cup ham, chopped*
 8 *small onions, peeled and left whole*
 8 *small whole mushrooms*
 1 *clove garlic, chopped*
¼ *teaspoon thyme*
 1 *bay leaf*
   Salt and freshly ground pepper, to taste
 1 *cup dry red wine*

Dredge chukar pieces with flour. Heat butter in a heavy skillet. Add chukar and brown on all sides (or brown in microwave browning dish, according to manufacturer's suggestions if desired).

Transfer chukar to large casserole. Add remaining ingredients. Cover tightly. Micro on 60 percent or bake for 18–20 minutes until meat is cooked through.

ORANGE GLAZED CHUKARS
Serves 2

2 chukars
½ orange, cut in half again
6 tablespoons frozen orange juice concentrate
3 tablespoons sugar
1 teaspoon ginger
½ teaspoon nutmeg

Place chukars in small casserole dish. Put orange segments inside birds. Wrap small pieces of aluminum foil around ends of legs to shield them. Make sure pieces of foil do not touch each other and are at least 1 inch from oven walls.

Mix orange juice concentrate, sugar, ginger, and nutmeg together in medium saucepan. (It will boil over if the container is too small.) Micro on high for 5 minutes. Spoon three-quarters of the mixture over the chukars. Cover tightly. Micro on 60 percent or bake for 12–13 minutes. Remove from oven and spoon remaining glaze over the birds.

Note: This is a very good way to cook chukars. In fact, the glaze could be used for most other game birds. It makes a delightful meal for guests. Be sure not to overcook the chukars—that is absolutely the worst thing you can do to these birds since there's not much fat on their little bodies.

CHUKAR TETRAZZINI
Serves 6

1½ cups cooked chukar, cubed
6 tablespoons butter
1 cup mushrooms
¼ cup flour
½ teaspoon freshly ground pepper
¾ cup chicken bouillon
1 cup heavy cream
1 package (7 ounces) spaghetti, cooked and drained
2 stalks celery, sliced
½ cup grated Parmesan cheese

In a small saucepan, micro 2 tablespoons of the butter 1 minute on high. Add mushrooms and micro on high for 4 minutes. Set aside.

In a large saucepan, micro 4 tablespoons butter on high 1 minute. Stir in flour and pepper. Stir in bouillon and cream. Micro on 70 percent or roast for 4–6 minutes until boiling. Allow to boil for 1 minute.

Stir in spaghetti, chukar, celery, and the mushrooms. Pour into 2-quart casserole. Sprinkle with cheese. Cover loosely. Micro on 80 percent or reheat for 4–5 minutes until heated through. (If you want the cheese topping browned, place it under the broiler in your oven for a few minutes.)

Note: I doubt you'll have many occasions to serve leftover game birds. My family usually devours them on the first go-around. But in case you do have leftover game birds, this is an excellent way to serve them. If they're reheated as they were when you originally cooked them, they'll often turn out dry. This recipe alleviates this problem.

Dove

It's not true that any wingshooter who brings home a bunch of doves for dinner is a genius behind a shotgun. Success on doves is proportional to the number of boxes of shells you went through to bag those doves!

The national average, I've read, is about two birds for five shells. That may be liberal. It's not that the nut behind the butt is incompetent, it's that the doves are hard to hit. They are fast and their flight patterns erratic.

Since doves are migratory game birds, in Nevada as in most other dove hunting states, we are pretty much dependent on the weather to dictate what kind of a dove season we'll have. In many parts of northwestern Nevada, the rain and/or an early frost chases the birds out of the area fast. You'd think the weatherman knew there was a hunting season opening.

The opening of dove season marks the first of the hunting season in Nevada. With the September 1 opener, the dove hunt has become a tradition of sorts here as well as in the South.

The tradition comes because the opener is on September 1, regardless of the day of the week. Anxious hunters, whether they're wingshooters or not, can't wait for the hunting season to open—*Any* hunting season—for an excuse to hit the fields. The opening of dove season marks the opener of a long autumn of chukar gunning, deer stalking, and waterfowl blasting. Only a few special hunts open before September 1 in Nevada, such as antelope and deer archery seasons, but for the hunter who looks forward to following the whim of hunting, of picking up his gun and taking to the field, the dove opener is the statewide excuse.

It doesn't matter whether you hunt mourning doves or whitewings, you'll enjoy hunting them as much as eating them. To ensure the best possible table fare, it's important to cool the birds down as quickly as possible. While this is important with all game birds, it is even more crucial with doves because the weather is often very warm when you hunt them.

While doves are small and it takes a few of them to satisfy an appetite, I enjoy eating them. In fact, they rank right up there in the top of my favorites.

Doves are excellent when prepared in the microwave. Of course some of the traditional fried recipes won't work, but for those sauced, smothered, and simmered recipes, doves are ideal.

Since the birds are so small it doesn't take much to cook them and microwave cooking is ideal. There are a number of recipes in this book for doves and I'm sure you'll enjoy trying them.

The breasts provide the biggest amount of meat on the birds, so many hunters fillet the breast meat and let the rest of the birds go, but I like to cook them whole and let the diners pick every tasty morsel from their skinny little legs.

CREAMY MUSHROOM DOVES

Serves 3–4

10 doves
8 tablespoons butter
Flour
3 cups mushrooms, sliced thickly
4 green onions, sliced
1½ cups heavy cream
2 tablespoons flour
Buttered noodles

In skillet, melt 4 tablespoons of the butter. Lightly dust doves with flour. Brown doves in melted butter. (Use microwave browning dish, if you wish.)

In a 2-quart casserole, melt 4 tablespoons butter on high 1 minute. Add mushrooms and onions. Stir well. Cover. Micro on high 4 minutes.

Pour in heavy cream. Stir well. Add doves. Stir to coat doves. Cover. Micro on 80 percent or reheat for 10 minutes. Stir.

Remove from microwave oven. Remove ½ cup of the creamy liquid. Stir in 2 tablespoons flour. Return mixture to doves. Stir well to combine.

Microwave on 80 percent for 3 minutes more. Stir well. Cover with aluminum foil and allow to sit for 5 minutes before serving. Serve over buttered noodles.

Note: This is one of my favorite recipes in the whole book. The sauce is delicious and very, very rich. Throw your calorie counter away and enjoy! The meat will be a little pink in this recipe, but the meat will certainly not be dry or tough if left that way.

DOVES OLE!
Serves 3–4

6 *doves*
4 *tablespoons olive oil*
Salt and ground pepper, to taste
½ *medium onion, chopped finely*
½ *green pepper, sliced thinly*
1 *clove garlic, minced*
1 *cup carrots, chopped finely*
1 *cup celery, chopped*
¾ *cup tomato juice*
1 *bay leaf*
¼ *cup black olives, sliced*

In a skillet, brown the doves in olive oil. Arrange doves in 8-inch square baking dish. Sprinkle salt and pepper over doves.

In a medium saucepan add a little fat from the skillet, onion, green pepper, and garlic and microwave on high for 4 minutes. Add the carrots, celery, tomato juice, and bay leaf. Stir well. Pour over doves.

Cover tightly. Micro on 80 percent for 13 minutes. Remove from the oven and add black olives. Cover with foil, shiny side down, for 5 minutes before serving.

SOUTHERN STYLE DOVES
Serves 3–4

 6 *doves*
¼ *cup flour*
   Salt and freshly ground pepper, to taste
 4 *tablespoons bacon fat*
½ *cup heavy cream*

Dust birds with flour and salt and pepper, to taste. Heat fat in skillet and brown the doves on all sides.

Transfer bacon fat and doves to microproof casserole. Pour the cream over the top. Microwave on 80 percent for 13–15 minutes or until the juices from the dove meat flow clearly.

Remove doves. Stir cream gravy well. Add some flour to thicken gravy, if desired.

PEACHY DOVES
Serves 3–4

6 *doves*
4 *tablespoons butter*
½ *medium onion, chopped*
1 *one-pound can peach halves packed in syrup,*
   drain but reserve ½ cup peach syrup
2 *teaspoons ginger*
1 *teaspoon powdered mustard*
2 *tablespoons cornstarch*

In microwave saucepan, melt butter on high 1 minute. Cook onion in butter 4 minutes on high. Add ½ cup reserved syrup, ginger, and mustard. Heat 1 minute on high.

In a 2-quart casserole, arrange doves and peach halves with the doves on the outside and peaches on the inside of the dish. Pour syrup mixture over the doves. Cover. Microwave at 80 percent for 15–18 minutes or until meat separates easily from the breast bone.

Remove the doves and peaches and arrange on a platter. Cover with aluminum foil while making sauce.

Add 2 tablespoons cornstarch to liquid, stirring well. Micro on high for 1 minute to thicken. Pour the gravy over the peaches and doves on the platter.

Note: The syrup gives this recipe a delicate, sweet taste—not thick or overpowering.

SAVORY DOVES
Serves 4–5

10 doves
¼ cup flour
3 tablespoons oil
1 tablespoon fresh parsley, minced
½ teaspoon paprika
2 tablespoons onion, minced
½ teaspoon seasoned salt
1 cup chicken bouillon or broth
¼ cup red wine

Dust the doves with the flour. In a stovetop skillet heat oil. Brown the doves in the skillet.

Mix remaining ingredients and pour into 3-quart casserole dish. Add the doves and stir well. Cover.

Micro on 80 percent power for 13–15 minutes, stirring once or twice during the cooking time. Remove the doves and thicken the sauce with a little flour if desired.

SOY SAUCED DOVES

Serves 4–5

10 doves
⅓ cup soy sauce
⅓ cup water
2 tablespoons sugar
1 tablespoon sherry
1 pinch anise
1 sliver of fresh or dry ginger

Place all ingredients except doves in 8-inch square baking dish. Micro on high 3–5 minutes or until boiling. Stir well. Micro sauce for 5 minutes more on 90 percent or simmer.

Add the doves and spoon the mixture over them. Micro on 80 percent for 13–15 minutes or until doves are cooked. Stir once or twice during cooking time.

Note: This recipe works equally well on chicken wings that can be served as hors d'oeuvres.

SPICY DOVES

Serves 4–5

10 doves
4 tablespoons butter
Salt and pepper, to taste
4 tablespoons olive oil
1 onion, chopped finely
2 cloves garlic, sliced
1 tablespoon parsley, finely chopped
1 green pepper, chopped
3 stalks celery, chopped
1 bay leaf
1 tablespoon Worcestershire sauce
½ teaspoon chili powder
1 tablespoon brown sugar
1 28-ounce can tomatoes
1 small can mushrooms, chopped

Rub the cavity of each bird with butter and salt and pepper.

In a heavy skillet place enough olive oil to cover the bottom of the skillet. Add the onion and garlic and sauté until lightly browned. Remove the onion and garlic to a medium microproof saucepan. Set aside. Add the birds and brown lightly on all sides adding more oil if necessary. Place browned birds in 2-quart casserole.

Add the remaining ingredients to the onions in the saucepan. Stir well. Micro on high for 15 minutes.

Add the doves and spoon the sauce over them. Cover tightly and micro on 60 percent for 13–15 minutes or until the doves are just barely cooked.

Note: This is a great dish to serve family members or guests.

Grouse

There are several different, quite distinct birds that wear the nameplate of a grouse: the regal ruffed grouse, the "fools hens" species, the pinnated grouse, the sharptail grouse and the large sage grouse. Each has its own kind of following and its own kind of reputation. While their following is usually largely dictated by the area the birds inhabit, their reputation is garnered by the habits of the different birds.

Sage grouse are large birds who look like freight trains trying to become airborne. The largest of the grouse family, the sage grouse provide excellent hunting for gunners in most of the western states. In Nevada, the sagehen hunting is usually excellent. Sage grouse are also found in the Dakotas, Idaho, Montana, Wyoming, Colorado, Utah, Washington, Oregon, and California.

While the bag limits are small and the seasons short in Nevada, the sage grouse hunt is becoming as much a tradition as the dove hunt has.

If you had to pick your favorite game bird, seldom would the sage grouse appear in that category. Since they're so large and they feed on sage, some hunters would definitely rather shoot them than eat them. Because limits are so small here, I know of hunters who stage sage grouse barbecues at their camp after a long day of hunting and thus no birds ever make it back to the kitchen.

The sage grouse is probably the nemesis of the game cook. Smart hunters say they only shoot young birds, but when they're blasting off the ground, I know I'm too busy figuring how to make them fly to my pattern to pick out the young birds from the older birds. The older birds, by the way, are tough, as anyone will tell you.

If you or your hunter brings home a tough bird, don't throw up your hands in panic. Roast it or cook it in any recipe you choose. If the meat is too tough, save it. Grind the meat or chop it and make a salad or sandwich filling out of it. Or use the chopped meat in a casserole.

Ruffed grouse are very elegant birds. They are wonderful to hunt and beautiful to look at. I like the way they strut, parading the fine colors of their tail fan. These birds are nonmigratory and are spread over a wide range in the United States.

Both blue grouse and spruce grouse are referred to as "fools hens," largely because they make such obvious targets for hunters. They will stand there and look at you while you draw a bead on them. Many hunters use .22s to hunt them, especially if the birds perch in the trees and won't flush. Even fair shots have a chance with these fools hens.

Sharptails and pinnated grouse or prairie chickens are other worthy quarry for grouse hunters. I'm envious of hunters who live in the states where these birds are hunted, since they're not currently found in the Silver State. Residents of the Plains States are lucky to have good populations of these birds to hunt.

Grouse provide excellent table fare aside from their fabulous hunting. Hunters in Nevada tell me their favorite game bird is the blue grouse and I can hardly argue with them.

No matter what your taste in grouse is, you'll find several recipes here to try on the grouse most likely to inhabit your neck of the woods.

ORANGE STUFFED GROUSE

Serves 4

4 grouse
Freshly ground pepper, to taste
1½ cups unseasoned stuffing mix
½ medium onion, chopped
3 tablespoons butter
3 tablespoons orange juice
¼ teaspoon rosemary
¼ teaspoon nutmeg
1 tablespoon orange peel, freshly grated
4 bacon slices

Sprinkle inside the cavity and the outsides of the birds with pepper. Mix stuffing mix, onion, butter, orange juice, rosemary and nutmeg. Spoon stuffing into grouse. Tie the legs of the grouse together with string.

Sprinkle orange peel over the outsides of the birds. Wrap with bacon slices. (Fasten with toothpicks, if necessary.)

Cover loosely with plastic wrap. Micro on 60 percent or bake for 15–18 minutes. Remove from oven and cover with foil, shiny side down, for 5 minutes before serving.

CURRIED SAGE GROUSE SALAD
Serves 6–8

4 cups cooked sage grouse, cut in chunks
3 cups cooked white rice
½ cup raw cauliflower, thinly sliced
½ cup creamy French salad dressing
1 cup mayonnaise
1½ teaspoons curry powder
1 teaspoon salt
¼ teaspoon pepper
½ cup milk
½ cup green peppers, diced
1 cup celery, thinly sliced
½ cup red onions, chopped
Romaine lettuce
¼ cup chutney
¼ cup hard boiled eggs, chopped
¼ cup peanuts
¼ cup pineapple chunks
¼ cup banana, diced
¼ cup coconut, shredded

Combine rice with cauliflower and French dressing and refrigerate at least 2 hours. Combine mayonnaise, curry powder, salt, and pepper. Slowly stir in the milk. Add sage grouse and toss. Refrigerate 2–3 hours.

Just before you're ready to serve, combine rice and sage grouse mixture, then add green pepper, celery, and onions. Serve on top of a platter lined with Romaine lettuce leaves. Serve with the chutney, chopped hard boiled eggs, peanuts, pineapple chunks, diced banana, and shredded coconut.

Note: This is a recipe devoted to those who don't know what to do with that tough, old sage grouse someone shot while in a frenzy or those leftovers of birds you can't bear to throw in the garbage. I think you'll enjoy serving this salad, even though it doesn't go near the microwave.

GROUSE AU VIN
Serves 4

4 grouse
1 cup chicken bouillon
1 cup dry white wine
Salt and freshly ground black pepper, to taste
1 tablespoon seasoned salt
½ teaspoon paprika
½ teaspoon parsley flakes
4 bacon strips

Pour the chicken bouillon into a 2-quart casserole dish. Stir in the wine.

Salt and pepper the birds inside and out. Sprinkle generously with seasoned salt. Place the birds back side down in the casserole. Dust the birds with paprika and parsley. Lay 1 strip of bacon over the breast portions of each bird.

Cover well. Micro on 60 percent power setting for 15–20 minutes or until the birds are just barely cooked. Remove from the oven and cover the dish with foil for several minutes before serving to complete the cooking. You should turn the casserole dish one-quarter turns once or twice during the cooking time to assure even cooking.

Pheasant

Pheasant probably ranks high up in the favorites list of most game connoisseurs with good reason. It is easy, however, to turn this delightful gourmet's starting place into something that resembles a piece of shoe leather.

One of the first times I ate pheasant, I was sorely disappointed. I was living in southern Idaho at the time, right in the middle of the state's corn belt and very near some of the best pheasant hunting ever.

When I first moved there, I was amused to see the big, gaudy birds parading down the dirt country roads (of course, not during hunting season). In Nevada, there aren't very many of the beautiful pheasant birds and I never tired of watching them whenever I had a chance.

I was in awe of pheasant the first time I hunted them and with good reason. I'd heard a lot about these impressive ringnecks. But what I hadn't read about or heard about was how my heart would pound when a big cock pheasant exploded at my feet trying to gain altitude so close it looked like he was trying to climb my pant leg. That, my friends, is when you learn to respect these wayward immigrants.

I'm jealous of those living in corn belt states where pheasants are somewhat prolific. Even if populations of ringnecks are down from their all-time highs, nearly every state with a water and a growing season sports good populations of pheasants–much better than Nevada's, I know.

Every hunter has his own favorite game bird. Dove hunters are convinced that doves provide the best targets for wingshooters, while grouse hunters say their particular brand of the sport is the most challenging. I have difficulty picking one favorite, but when it comes to the beauty contest, the elegant ringneck wins hands down.

The beautiful ringneck is one of the tops in the culinary department, too. But the first Idaho pheasant I ate was so overcooked, I couldn't figure out why everyone was so impressed with pheasants. It was dry and it was tasteless. It just goes to show that game can be overcooked using conventional methods, not just in the microwave oven.

Traditionally, roasting the pheasant has been *the* way to cook the bird. Of course, it is better to roast a young bird that is unlikely to be tough. An older bird will work better in recipes where there's liquid to simmer into the birds.

Don't be frightened away by the microwave when you want to cook grandiose birds like the pheasant. Don't let the microwave intimidate you. It works very well on pheasants. If you don't believe it, try roasting one bird in the microwave. Except for the browning part, you'll be pleased with the results, I guarantee. You can solve the problem of no browning on the skin by buttering the skin of the pheasant and sticking it under the broiler until browned. It works just fine and if you're short of time, I'd use the roasting recipe I've got here. If you've got plenty of time, use conventional methods of cooking. The microwave is not the cure-all in the kitchen.

When roasting a bird in the microwave, I take the time to shield the ends of the legs with aluminum foil so the legs won't overcook and dry out. This tip will come in handy when you cook pheasant.

CHEESY CHEDDAR PHEASANT
Serves 2–3

1 pheasant, quartered
1 can (11 ounces) cheddar cheese soup
½ cup buttermilk
1 tablespoon Worcestershire sauce
¾ teaspoon salt
½ medium onion, chopped
1 clove garlic, minced
1 cup mushrooms, sliced
Buttered noodles or spinach noodles

Mix soup, buttermilk, Worcestershire sauce, salt, onion, garlic, and mushrooms. Stir well.

Arrange pheasant pieces in microproof casserole. Cover with sauce. Cover.

Micro on high 5 minutes. Cook 15–20 minutes on bake or medium setting, until juices are no longer pink. Stir sauce and rearrange pheasant pieces once or twice during cooking.

Be careful not to pierce the skin of the pheasant while turning the pieces or stirring. By not piercing the skin you won't lose any of the bird's precious juices.

Serve pheasant and sauce over buttered noodles or spinach noodles. Sprinkle with paprika.

SOUPED UP PHEASANT
Serves 2–4

1 pheasant, quartered
3 tablespoons oil
2 stalks celery, sliced
1 onion, chopped
1 green pepper, chopped
1 can chicken and rice soup
1 can cream of mushroom soup
½ teaspoon garlic powder
½ teaspoon onion powder
2 teaspoons parsley flakes
Rice

Heat oil in heavy skillet. Brown the pheasant pieces on all sides. Place the pheasant in a 3-quart casserole.

In small saucepan, mix celery, onion, and green pepper. Add a tablespoon or two of water. Cover well and micro on high for 5 minutes. Mix in the remaining ingredients and stir well.

Pour the vegetable and soup mixture over the pheasant pieces and stir well to combine. Cover well. Micro on high for 5 minutes. Reduce power to 60 percent or bake, and micro for 15–20 minutes until the juices of the pheasant run clear. Stir several times during cooking to evenly cook the bird.

Serve on a bed of rice.

ROAST PHEASANT
Serves 2

1 pheasant
Freshly ground black pepper
Salt, to taste
1 bay leaf
1 clove garlic
Few celery leaves
2 tablespoons butter, melted

Sauce:
½ cup consommé
2 tablespoons flour
2 tablespoons butter, melted
3 tablespoons Madeira wine

Sprinkle the inside and the outside of the pheasant with the pepper. Add salt, if you wish. Place the bay leaf, garlic, and celery leaves on the inside of the pheasant. Tie the legs together with string.

Insert temperature probe or microproof meat thermometer. Cover the bird loosely. Micro on 70 percent or roast until the temperature reaches 170–180 degrees, until the juices from the bird run clear.

Remove from the microwave and brush with butter. Brown under the broiler of your conventional oven.

Sauce: Add the consommé to the drippings from the roast pan. Micro on high for 2 minutes. Blend the flour with the butter and stir into the gravy a little at a time. Micro on 80 percent or reheat for 2–3 minutes until thickened. Stir well, then add the Madeira wine.

Serve the pheasant with wine sauce.

CREAMY PHEASANT
Serves 2–3

1 pheasant, quartered
3 tablespoons olive oil
1 tablespoon Worcestershire sauce
3 tablespoons butter
½ medium onion, chopped
2 stalks celery, chopped
1 cup mushrooms, sliced
1 can cream of chicken soup
½ cup dry white wine
Paprika

Heat oil in heavy skillet. Brown pheasant on all sides. Place the pheasant in a 9-inch square baking dish.

In a small saucepan, micro butter 1 minute on high. Add onions, celery, and mushrooms. Micro on high 5 minutes. Stir in soup and wine. Pour over the pheasant. Sprinkle liberally with paprika.

Micro on high for 5 minutes. Reduce to 70 percent and micro for 15–18 minutes or until the juices from the pheasant run clear. Cover with foil for 3–5 minutes to finish cooking.

PHEASANT AND MUSHROOMS
Serves 2–3

1 pheasant, quartered
Salt, to taste
Freshly ground black pepper, to taste
4 tablespoons olive oil
2 tablespoons butter
1 pound mushrooms, sliced
½ medium onion, chopped
⅓ cup tomato sauce
½ cup parsley, chopped
Buttered noodles

Sprinkle pheasant with salt and pepper. Heat oil in heavy frying pan and brown pheasant on all sides. Place pheasant in an 8-inch square baking dish or one large enough to hold the bird.

Place butter in medium saucepan and micro on high for 1 minute. Add mushrooms and onion and micro on high for 5 minutes. Add tomato sauce and parsley.

Pour over the pheasants. Cover tightly. Micro on high for 5 minutes. Micro on 70 percent or roast for 15–18 minutes until the pheasant's juices run clear.

Serve over buttered noodles.

Quail

Quail hunting is steeped in tradition. Most of the tradition surrounds the ever-popular bobwhite quail. Why do you enjoy hunting bobwhites? Is it seeing your dogs working a covey? Is it the way the birds explosively rise when flushed? Or is it the bird's pretty little markings?

I reckon a mixture of those things endears the bobwhite to the hearts of hunters fortunate enough to live in bobwhite territory or those with enough foresight to plan hunting vacations in bobwhite land.

The rest of us, living in country with no bobwhites, have become familiar with the bobwhite's close cousins: the Gambel's quail, the scaled quail, the Mountain quail, the California or valley quail, and the Harlequin or Mearns quail.

I happen to like hunting the quail with the top-knot. Often the California or valley quail I hunt run mightily through the brush before flushing. Their calls send shivers up and down my spine, especially when I can hear them and can't see them.

Nearly everything you'll read about field care for quail will mention that cooling them immediately is of utmost importance in preserving their excellent taste. Quail hunting in the West can be done during some pretty warm days and the temperature of the outdoors will greatly influence how you should treat these delicate birds. Some rudimentary cleaning will help assure sweet meat when you return home.

Most hunters will use vests with big game pockets to stow their birds until they get back to their vehicle. This isn't ideal because there is little ventilation in these game pockets, but the birds will usually be alright if you clean them first. Some people then put each bird in individual plastic bags, but I wouldn't recommend this because the birds will undoubtedly remain warm in those bags, even if cleaned.

Once you get back to your vehicle and store the birds in your ice chest, you've done all you can to ensure the quality taste of your birds remains just that.

When you get home, a more thorough cleaning job is in order. Some people skin their birds and some pluck them. I usually skin small birds because I can find very small benefit in plucking such small birds. After you're done with your cleaning chores, rinse the birds well and pat them dry. Then you can prepare them for dinner or wrap them in suitable freezer wrap.

This beloved bird is best cooked as simply as possible. Most game connoisseurs like them fried or Southern-style. I'm sure you'll find a recipe or two here to suit your tastes. If not, the cooking times for these birds are just a little longer than for doves or a little shorter than for grouse, so you can filch recipes from those sections if they appeal to you.

QUAIL WITH GRAPES
Serves 2

4 quail
4 slices bacon
2 tablespoons butter
Salt, to taste
Freshly ground black pepper, to taste
¼ cup brandy
¼ cup water
¼ pound green grapes
4 slices French bread, toasted and buttered

Cover the breasts with bacon and tie with string around the body to hold the bacon slices in place. Brush with butter and sprinkle with salt and pepper. Pour the brandy over the quail and touch with lighted match to flame.

Place the quail in casserole dish just large enough to hold them. Add ¼ cup water. Cover tightly. Micro on 60 percent for 15–18 minutes or until the juices from the birds run clear. Rearrange the birds halfway through the cooking time so birds cook evenly.

Remove the birds to a plate and cover them with aluminum foil shiny side down to finish cooking.

Remove fat from the casserole, reserving the other juices and sediment. Micro the reserved juices on 80 percent for 2 minutes.

Peel the grapes and add grapes to the juices. Stir well. Micro on 50 percent for 1 minute.

Garnish serving platter with pieces of toasted bread. Place the birds on top of the toast and surround the birds with grapes. Serve leftover cooking juices separately.

QUAIL IN PARMESAN SAUCE
Serves 4

8 quail
Salt, to taste
Freshly ground black pepper, to taste
5 tablespoons butter
2 tablespoons flour
¾ cup light cream
⅓ cup Parmesan cheese
3 egg yolks, beaten
½ cup fresh bread crumbs

Season the quail with salt and pepper. In a heavy skillet, melt half the butter and brown the quail on both sides.

In a microproof saucepan, micro remaining butter on high 1 minute. Add flour and stir with a whisk until blended. In a separate saucepan micro cream on high 3–5 minutes or until boiling. Add all at once to flour/butter mixture, stirring until blended. Add one tablespoon of cheese to the mixture. When the cheese is melted, stir in the egg yolks.

Sprinkle the bottom of a glass baking dish with ¼ cup of the cheese. Arrange the quail on the cheese and spoon the sauce over the top of the birds. Cover tightly. Micro on 60 percent or bake for 15–18 minutes.

QUAIL MARSALA
Serves 4

8 quail
3 tablespoons oil
¼ cup butter
¼ cup Canadian bacon, chopped
1 small onion, chopped
1 tablespoon flour
½ cup chicken bouillon
4 tablespoons Marsala wine
1 bay leaf
8 slices French bread, toasted and buttered

Heat oil in skillet and brown the birds in the oil. Place the birds in a large baking dish.

In a small saucepan, micro butter on high for 1 minute. Add the Canadian bacon and onion. Micro on high for 5 minutes. Stir in flour, the bouillon, the Marsala, and the bay leaf. Pour over the quail.

Micro on 80 percent for 10–12 minutes. Place the quail on pieces of toasted French bread and cover with the Marsala mixture.

QUAIL IN MUSHROOMS
Serves 4–5

8 quail
3 tablespoons oil
1 teaspoon rosemary
1 teaspoon sage
8 slices bacon
1 cup pearl onions, peeled
¼ cup butter
5 slices bacon, chopped
2 cups mushrooms, sliced
½ cup dry white wine

Wash and dry the quail. Heat oil in a heavy skillet and brown birds. Cool birds slightly and put ⅛ teaspoon rosemary and ⅛ teaspoon sage in each bird. Put 1 slice of bacon in each cavity.

Place onions on plate in microwave and micro on high for 3 minutes. Melt butter in casserole and add the onions and bacon. Micro on high for 3–5 minutes or until bacon is golden. Add mushrooms and micro for 5 minutes on high.

In a casserole large enough to hold the birds, place the vegetables in the bottom and place the quail on the top. Pour the wine over the top of the birds. Cover loosely and micro on 70 percent or roast for 10–12 minutes until birds are cooked through.

Woodcock and Jacksnipe

Woodcocks are about as foreign to western hunters as chukar are to easterners and southerners. Robert Elman writes in his book *1001 Hunting Tips*, "The best advice I can give them [hunters who have never seen woodcocks] is to move. . . ."

Also called the timberdoodle (which in my mind is such a romantic name—I kind of like that), the woodcock is a migratory bird and is protected by federal regulations.

While I'll admit I've never seen a timberdoodle (the recipes in this book come from friends), I would recognize one anywhere by its long bill. They use their long bills—the lady timberdoodle's is longer—to dig in the ground for worms.

The woodcock is a close family member of the snipe and recipes included here will also work on the snipe bird.

Hunting woodcocks is becoming very popular, even though the hunt takes place in areas most sane wingshooters dare to tread. Woodcocks live in slough bottoms overgrown with willows and heavy, brushy undergrowth.

Bird dogs work well on woodcocks because it is often necessary to put the tightly roosted birds in the air. Like doves, they are extremely fast targets and their quick acceleration will astound most wingshooters.

Because the birds are so small, many hunters make a personal decision to use only the breasts. But you can serve the entire bird without trying to remove the breast only.

Recipes for doves will also work on these birds and the cooking times are very close to the same.

The jacksnipe is spread over a much wider range than the woodcock, so I suspect there's a little more hunter interest in snipe.

The snipe also has a long, pointed bill for eating. Its diet consists of a wider variety of insects than does the woodcock's. Snipe use wet grounds for their feeding activities, so the best places to look for these birds are along sloughs and marshlands.

The best method of hunting snipe is walking them up. Dogs are infrequently used on jacksnipe. This game bird is greatly overlooked by hunters.

BRANDIED WOODCOCK
Serves 2–3

4 woodcocks
4 tablespoons butter
½ medium onion, finely chopped
2 tablespoons brandy
¼ cup beef bouillon
Freshly ground pepper
2 cups baby carrots
2 tablespoons flour
Fresh parsley, chopped

In a large skillet melt butter. Add onions and cook for 2–3 minutes. Add woodcocks and brown on all sides. Pour in brandy and flame with a match.

Pour woodcock mixture into a 2-quart casserole. Stir in bouillon, pepper, and baby carrots. Cover. Micro on 80 percent power for 8–10 minutes. Remove the woodcocks and the carrots from the mixture to a warm platter and cover with foil. Add 2 tablespoons flour to the liquid and stir well.

Return the sauce to the microwave and cook for 3 minutes at 80 percent. Pour the sauce over the woodcocks (not over the carrots). Garnish the carrots with freshly chopped parsley.

WOODCOCK IN WINE SAUCE
Serves 4–5

8 woodcocks
Salt and freshly ground black pepper, to taste
Flour
6 tablespoons butter
½ medium onion, finely chopped
½ cup celery, thinly sliced
2 cups chicken bouillon
¼ cup dry white wine
1 teaspoon tarragon

Roux:

2 tablespoons flour
2 tablespoons butter

Spinach noodles, buttered
Mushrooms, cooked and buttered

Sprinkle woodcocks inside and out, with salt and pepper to taste. Dust with flour and brown on all sides in 4 tablespoons melted butter. In 3-quart casserole, microwave 2 tablespoons butter on high for 1 minute. Add onions and celery and micro on high for 3 minutes. Add chicken bouillon, wine, and tarragon. Micro on high 3–5 minutes or until boiling.

In the meantime, make a roux on stovetop with 2 tablespoons each of flour and butter. When lightly browned add a little of the simmering liquid and mix thoroughly. Add roux to wine mixture a little at a time. Stir well.

Add the woodcocks and stir well. Micro on 80 percent for 14–16 minutes or until woodcocks are almost finished cooking.

Remove from microwave and cover with aluminum foil, shiny side down. Allow to sit 5 minutes before serving on a bed of spinach noodles with fresh, cooked and buttered mushrooms.

Waterfowl

Duck

Duck meat seems to have about the same kind of reputation as antelope meat—either you love to eat it or you hate to eat it. Whether it's waterfowl, upland game, or big game, reputation of game meat, I believe, is heavily dependent on how it is taken care of in the field. The important factor is the same regardless of the bird or animal. It is critical to cool the meat off as soon as possible.

With waterfowl, the weather may make all the difference in the world to how your birds will taste. If it's cold outside, the timing of the cleaning chores on the birds is not as critical as it is in warm weather. The low temperature may take care of the cooling process for you. If it's hot outside, some in-the-field care will help things along. I think it's important to at least gut the birds as soon as possible. Now I guarantee I won't be the one doing it when the birds are still flying and the action is hot as a dry skillet, but once things have slowed down, you might work on a few ducks at a time.

There's one thing you'll have to get used to if you're going to eat ducks. Ducks taste like ducks taste like ducks. If you don't care for the taste of them, no soaking method or roasting method or marinade or sauce will change that. Of course, some ducks taste different than others. I wouldn't serve any of the diving ducks to the wife of my husband's boss, especially if she was not a game aficionado. But there are other more tasty ducks she might appreciate. As a general rule, puddler ducks, since they feed more heavily on aquatic plant life than do divers, are usually less gamey.

A couple of seasons ago, when a slim day of hunting only produced two teal, I defrosted a mallard and roasted the mallard and teal together. Everyone agreed the teal were better tasting. Of course, that's only a matter of taste, too. I enjoy all kinds of ducks, but I recognize they all have their individual tastes.

The roast duck is a standard of game cooking. I have had mixed results with roasting ducks in the microwave. No, I haven't had the problem with dry game as you would believe is common in the microwave. I like to use the temperature probe when roasting meat. Occasionally the temperature probe will register the temperature I believe is best, but the meat isn't cooked as much as I like it. You may find this to be true with recipes you try in the microwave. The nice thing about the microwave is the problem is usually corrected in a few short minutes.

When roasting ducks in the microwave, once you've reached the recommended temperature, make a small incision near the breastbone to check the doneness of the meat. If it's not cooked enough to suit you, return it to the oven for a few minutes.

I am not one who likes my duck meat cooked well-done. I like the juices in the breast, when checked as above, to run just a little pink. If you like your duck meat well-done, you might also have to add some time.

Some of the recipes in this section call for duck breasts. Often hunters will cut the breasts out of the duck and forget the rest. This is a good way to quickly cook ducks or to add duck meat to a variety of recipes. If you do this, I can't advocate throwing away the rest of the bird. Wrap it and put it in the freezer to use in a soup at a later date. I like to get the most mileage out of my game and this is one way to do it.

With grocery bills as high as they are, we hunters appreciate any breaks we can get by adding game to our larder. I don't like the thought of not fully utilizing any and all edible portions of game. The fish and game departments around the country aren't tickled about wasting game, either. Just check the "wanton waste of game" section of your state's hunting regulations for the penalty this carries.

Many hunters grew up with parents teaching them the "you shoot it, you eat it" method of hunting. Besides, half the fun of hunting is coming up with new ways to prepare nearly any kind of game meat. You wouldn't be reading this cookbook if you didn't subscribe to that thought, now would you?

It's hard to pick my favorite recipe in this section of duck recipes. I have always seen many recipes for ducks in cream and once I tried it, I knew I'd have to fashion a recipe to be included in this book. Ducks in Apple and Cream Sauce is one of my favorites, especially since the taste is so unusual.

I should mention that one of my favorite soup recipes is the one I devised called Easy Duck Soup. This recipe will pass the taste buds of even the most squeamish game eater, unless he or she hates onions.

The recipe for barbecued duck breasts is also first-rate. If you want to put your microwave aside, you can cook them over the coals, making it a true barbecued dinner.

Ducks provide splendid eating and there are many, many ways of preparing them. You're not stuck with just the traditional "stuffed with apples and onions and roasted" affair. While I'm not discounting that very excellent way of preparing ducks, there are many new recipes around to tempt waterfowl eaters. The fun doesn't have to end once you've left the blind.

CHERRY SAUCED DUCK BREASTS
Serves 3–4

2½–3 pounds large duck breasts (about 8)
1 onion, sliced thinly
2 oranges, separated into segments
1 cup Tangy Cherry Sauce (see p. 172)

In a 2-quart casserole, combine duck breasts with onions and oranges. Pour sauce over the duck breast mixture.

Cover well. Micro on 70 percent or roast 15–18 minutes. Let sit 5 minutes before serving to finish cooking.

Pour leftover cherry sauce over duck breasts before serving. Pass the remaining sauce at the table. (The oranges and onions can be removed if so desired.)

DUCKS WITH BACON AND ONIONS
Serves 3–4

Breasts from 7 or 8 large ducks
½ pound bacon, cut in thirds
1 medium onion, cut in rings
Salt and freshly ground pepper
Flour

In a large casserole, combine bacon and onions. Dust with salt and pepper. Cover. Micro on high for 6 minutes, stirring once or twice.

Dust duck breasts lightly with flour. Add duck breasts to onion and bacon mixture. Micro on 60 percent for 18–19 minutes or until juices run clear. Stir once or twice while cooking. Remove from oven and cover with aluminum foil shiny side down to finish cooking for at least 5 minutes.

Note: I think the red meat from duck breasts tastes very similar to liver. One of the traditional ways to cook liver is with bacon and onions.

In case you have small ducks in your freezer, don't bother to debone the breasts. Just substitute the same number of small ducks for the large breast pieces. You may have to adjust the time, though, so be careful. I've cooked teal this way and found them delicious. You don't have to shoot mallards each time out to enjoy a good duck dinner.

SPINACH CASSEROLED DUCK BREASTS
Serves 3–4

Breasts from 7 or 8 large ducks
⅓ cup olive oil
1 bunch green onions, sliced
  Salt and freshly ground pepper
1 10-ounce package frozen spinach, thawed and drained thoroughly
½ pound ricotta cheese

In stovetop skillet, heat olive oil. Add green onions and sauté lightly. Add duck breasts. Brown on both sides. Drain duck breasts and onions. Place in microproof 8-inch square casserole dish. Dust with salt and pepper.

In medium bowl, mix spinach and ricotta. Spread mixture over duck breasts. Cover tightly.

Micro at 60 percent or bake for 18 minutes. Remove from oven and cover with aluminum foil, shiny side down, at least 5 minutes before serving.

EASY DUCK SOUP
Serves 4

Breasts from 4 or 5 ducks, boned and chopped in 1-inch cubes
4 *tablespoons butter*
1 *onion, chopped*
3 *cups beef bouillon*
2 *bay leaves*
½ *teaspoon garlic powder*
Salt and freshly ground pepper, to taste
1 *cup soup mix or barley*

Melt butter in skillet. Add onions and cook for 3–4 minutes or until onion is soft. Add duck breasts and cook, stirring, until duck breasts are browned on all sides.

Transfer duck meat and onions to a 2-quart casserole. Add 2 cups of the bouillon and seasonings. Cover. Micro on high 3 minutes. Reduce heat to 50 percent or simmer and cook for 20 minutes.

Add soup mix or barley and more beef bouillon. Cover loosely. Micro on high 3 minutes. Reduce heat to 50 percent or simmer and cook for 20 minutes. Allow to sit for a few minutes before serving.

Note: This is one of my favorite soup recipes. The soup is very hearty and is great served with big chunks of fresh, warm French bread.

DUCKS IN APPLE AND CREAM SAUCE
Serves 4

2 *large ducks or 4 small ducks*
1 *3-ounce package cream cheese*
4 *tablespoons butter*
3 *tablespoons bourbon*
½ *cup apple juice*
4 *cooking apples, cored and sliced thinly*
½ *cup golden raisins*
½ *cup heavy cream*

Spread cavity of ducks with cream cheese. Tie the legs of the ducks together with string. Melt butter in skillet. Add the ducks and brown on all sides.

Place ducks in 2-quart casserole. Pour bourbon over the tops and sides of the ducks. Touch with lighted match. When the flames die down, add juice around the ducks. Place temperature probe in duck breast making certain you don't touch any bones. Cover loosely.

Microwave on 60 percent or bake until the temperature reaches 180 degrees. Prick the skin of the duck and baste with the juice once during cooking time.

Add apples, raisins, and heavy cream. Micro on 60 percent for 8–10 minutes more. Serve with apples and raisins around the ducks. Spoon the sauce over the top and serve extra sauce to pass around.

Note: I've noticed many game cookbooks with recipes for ducks in cream sauce and I thought it was an unusual way to serve duck, so I adapted a recipe for the microwave. The sauce is delicious and the flavoring delicately accentuates the flavor of the ducks.

DUCKS WITH SAUERKRAUT AND APPLES
Serves 4

2 large ducks or 4 small ones
   Salt and freshly ground pepper, to taste
1 large cooking apple, cored and sliced
1 cup sauerkraut, drained
1 teaspoon caraway seeds
½ medium onion, chopped
2 tablespoons apple or currant jelly

Salt and pepper inside cavities and outsides of ducks. Place them in large casserole.

Combine apple slices, sauerkraut, caraway seeds, and onion. Divide the stuffing in half (or quarters) and stuff the ducks. Tie the legs of the ducks together and place them breasts up in the casserole. Brush outside skin with jelly.

Insert temperature probe in breast and microwave at 60 percent until temperature reaches 180 degrees. Check to see if the bird is almost done. Remove from the oven and cover with foil for 5 minutes before serving.

BARBECUED DUCK BREASTS
Serves 3–4

Breasts from 4 or 5 large ducks, boned
¼ *cup white vinegar*
½ *cup tomato paste*
3 *tablespoons brown sugar, packed*
1 *teaspoon onion, minced*
1 *teaspoon chili powder*
1 *teaspoon Worcestershire sauce*
½ *teaspoon freshly ground pepper*
½ *teaspoon dry mustard*

Mix the vinegar, tomato paste, brown sugar, minced onion, chili powder, Worcestershire sauce, pepper, and mustard. Stir well. Pour over the ducks in a medium bowl and refrigerate 4–5 hours.

Remove breasts from the sauce and arrange in a single layer in a glass baking dish. Cover loosely. Microwave on 80 percent or reheat for 9–13 minutes. Remove from the microwave and cover with foil for 5 minutes before serving.

Meanwhile, microwave leftover sauce on high for 1–2 minutes or until heated through.

Serve the duck breasts with extra sauce passed around.

Note: This is a good way to introduce the taste of ducks to someone who thinks game bird meat tastes too gamey. The seasonings mask any strong flavor the ducks might have as they enhance it.

Goose

I know there are some who would disagree with me but I think the goose is the most elegant creature a game hunter can bring home to grace his table. The Christmas goose is a tradition I've always thought very highly of and is one I'm going to begin in our family next Christmas season. I can't think of a more gratifying time for providing for your family than during the Christmas season.

I'll have to tell you that I was a little apprehensive when I first tried roasting a goose in the microwave. In fact, I was beginning to believe everything I'd heard about the microwave not being the oven to roast or bake in. I believed it so hard that I wrote the introduction to this book before I'd even tried roasting very much. Once I received my hands-on experience, though, I had to go back and rewrite my earlier opinion.

I wrote that you wouldn't find many recipes for roasts in this cookbook because the microwave just doesn't do a good job on them. I've found since writing it that my statement was heavily influenced by others who discount the microwave.

The first time I cooked a goose in the microwave was in the middle of the summer and we didn't have one in the freezer. Our friends, John and Kristin Lee, had a goose they'd been saving in their freezer, so we pooled our assets.

When they arrived at our house with the goose, I stuffed it and put it in the microwave. I then served cocktails and hors d'oeuvres as we awaited the results. The bird was done in about forty minutes. My guests were not starving to death. My kitchen wasn't overheated and the best part about it was that the bird turned out just great. You'd never know, except by the lack of a brown skin, that the bird was cooked in the microwave. The meat of the bird was juicy and tender, not unlike the results of a conventional oven. I really was surprised and very pleased at the results.

Of course on Christmas day, when I want the aroma of roast goose wafting throughout my home, I'll cook in the conventional oven. But my guests don't want to wait for hours for the goose to cook and I don't blame them, because I don't either.

Goose, like most waterfowl, works well with sweet or pungent spices and flavors. Most fruits work well in a stuffing or as a sauce for goose. There are several sauces included in this section, and still others in the section of Sauces, Butters, and Marinades, that nicely complement waterfowl.

My favorite way to prepare goose is stuffed with some sort of dressing, served with a sweet, pungent sauce alongside the goose. If you have any leftovers the next day, place the pieces of goose meat on a plate, cover them liberally with the sauce, and microwave on your reheat setting for several minutes to breathe life back into your meal.

You might have other sorts of recipes for leftovers that will adapt well to the microwave. I've never had enough leftovers to experiment with.

Hunting geese is an experience. It's really nice if you know someone or know someone who knows someone who owns some cropland where you could hunt. Most of the best hunting around occurs when the birds are coming in to feeding areas. But of course, if you don't know anyone, your next best bet is to scout feeding areas that the geese have been using and politely ask the rancher or farmer if you could hunt on his land. Remember: when entering any kind of land, whether it's private or public, we hunters have a tarnished image already. If we don't act courteously and respectfully of the land, we only further tarnish that image. Act as you would like to be treated. If the landowner turns you down, which he has every right to do, remain pleasant and courteous and give a hearty "thanks anyway."

In my home state of Nevada we're in a lucky position. Eighty-seven percent of the land in Nevada is public land. While this is terrific, one of the problems with it is that Nevada has proven to be an attractive place for people to relocate their families. Nevada is one of the fastest growing states in the country. Because of this, we have to share that land with many more people who once lived somewhere else.

It may not be long before we don't have all that public, available land anymore. Then we'll need to ask the landowners' permission to hunt private land. If we don't respect them now, we're going to lose their support in the future.

GOOSE WITH APRICOT AND PRUNE STUFFING
Serves 4–6

1 goose

Stuffing:

3 cups cornbread stuffing mix
½ teaspoon sage
½ teaspoon rosemary
¼ teaspoon thyme
½ cup pitted prunes, chopped
½ cup dried apricots, chopped
1 tablespoon butter, melted
2 eggs
½ cup milk

Sauce:

1 cup apricot preserves
¼ cup Burgundy wine

Stuffing: Mix the stuffing ingredients together and stir well to wet all ingredients. Stuff the goose loosely with the stuffing. If there's any stuffing left over, cook it in a covered casserole separate from the goose.

Place goose in 9×13–inch baking dish or one large enough to hold the bird. Truss the bird if desired and tie the legs together with string. Place small pieces of aluminum foil around the leg tips to protect them from overcooking. Make sure pieces of foil do not touch each other and are at least 1 inch from oven walls.

Mix together the apricot preserves and the Burgundy wine. Spread about 2–3 tablespoons over the top of the bird. Place temperature probe in the thickest part of the meat between the leg and the breast. Cover loosely with plastic wrap.

Micro on 70 percent or roast until temperature reaches 180–185 degrees. Turn bird over halfway through cooking. Make a slit between leg and body of goose to test for doneness. Add more time if desired. Remove from the oven and cover tightly with aluminum foil, shiny side down, for at least 5 minutes.

Meanwhile, place the rest of the apricot sauce in the microwave and micro on high 2–3 minutes or until heated through. Serve the sauce with the goose.

Note: I just finished cooking this for company and it was just delicious. No one would ever know it was cooked in the microwave. The sauce is excellent and the stuffing is just the right touch. I served it with a green salad loaded with tomatoes and peppers and sautéed zucchini fresh from my garden.

GOOSE STUFFED WITH RAISINS AND ORANGE SAUCE

Serves 4–6

1 goose, rinsed and patted dry

Stuffing:

½ cup butter
2 stalks celery, sliced
½ medium onion, chopped
3 cups cornbread stuffing mix
2 eggs
½ cup milk
¼ teaspoon rosemary
¼ teaspoon marjoram
1 cup dark raisins

Sauce:

2 cups orange juice
¼ cup sugar
1 tablespoon cornstarch
½ teaspoon ground cinnamon
¼ teaspoon ground nutmeg
3 cloves

In a large bowl or casserole, micro butter 1 minute on high. Add the celery and the onion and micro on high for 4 minutes. Stir in the remaining stuffing ingredients and stir well to combine. Stuff the goose lightly with the dressing.

Sauce: In a 2-quart saucepan, mix all sauce ingredients and micro on high for 3–5 minutes or until boiling. Reduce power to 50 percent or simmer and micro for 3–4 minutes until sauce thickens. Stir once or twice during the cooking time. Discard the cloves.

Place the goose in a 9×13-inch baking dish or one large enough to hold it. Truss goose, if desired, and tie legs together. Shield tips of legs with small pieces of aluminum foil. Make sure pieces of foil do not touch each other and are at least 1 inch from oven walls. Spoon 2–3 tablespoons of sauce over goose. Insert temperature probe in thickest part of goose between the leg and breast. Cover loosely.

Micro on 70 percent or roast until the temperature of the goose reaches 180–185 degrees. This normally will take between 30–40 minutes. Turn the bird over halfway through cooking time.

Serve the remaining sauce with the goose.

WILD RICE AND SAUSAGE STUFFED GOOSE
Serves 4–6

1 goose, rinsed and patted dry

Stuffing:
½ pound pork or game sausage, cooked
3 cups cooked wild rice
2 tablespoons butter, melted
3 stalks celery, sliced
½ medium onion, chopped

2 tablespoons butter, melted
1 teaspoon sage

Mix all the ingredients of the stuffing together in a large bowl. Stir well to combine.

Loosely stuff goose with stuffing. Truss the goose, if desired, and tie the legs together with string. Shield tips of legs with small pieces of aluminum foil to prevent overcooking. Make sure pieces of foil do not touch each other and are at least 1 inch from oven walls.

Mix together the melted butter and the sage and brush over the outside of the goose. Insert the temperature probe of your microwave in the thickest part of the goose between the leg and the breast. Micro on 70 percent or roast until the temperature reaches 180–185 degrees. This normally takes about 30–40 minutes, depending on the size of the bird. Turn the goose over halfway through cooking time to ensure complete cooking.

APPLE ORCHARD GOOSE
Serves 4–6

1 goose, rinsed and dried

Stuffing:
3 cups cooking apples, cored and sliced thinly
3 tablespoons lemon juice
1 cup golden raisins
½ cup sugar
1 teaspoon ground cinnamon
¼ teaspoon ground nutmeg
2 or 3 cardamom seeds, crushed

Sauce:
1 cup apple jelly
2–3 tablespoons cider vinegar, to taste

Mix all the ingredients of the stuffing together. Stir well.

Lightly stuff the goose with the apple mixture. Tie the legs of the goose together if desired. Place small pieces of aluminum foil over the tips of the legs to prevent overcooking. Make sure pieces of foil do not touch each other and are at least 1 inch from oven walls. Place the bird in baking dish.

Mix the sauce ingredients together and spoon 2–3 tablespoons of the sauce over the bird. Insert the temperature probe in the thickest part of the meat between the leg and the breast. Cover loosely. Micro on 70 percent or roast until the temperature reaches 180–185 degrees. This will usually take between 30–40 minutes depending on the size of the goose. Turn the goose over halfway through cooking time.

Remove the goose from the oven, remove the probe, and cover tightly with aluminum foil to finish cooking while you heat the sauce. Leave the goose covered for at least 5 minutes before serving.

Heat the remaining sauce on high for 3–4 minutes or until heated thoroughly. Serve the sauce with the goose.

Small Game

Rabbit

When it comes right down to it, every hunter who's ever taken to the field has probably killed a rabbit or two somewhere in his lifetime. That's one thing we have in common whether we live on the California coast or the bayous of Louisiana. From New York to Florida there have been plenty of bunnies taken.

Now I didn't say all these bunnies were cottontails, did I? A fair number of hunters were weaned on black-tailed jacks while those lucky enough can fill their bag with snowshoe hares. Probably the most common of the eating bunnies is the cottontail.

While there have probably been more cottontails harvested by hunters than any other game animal, don't get to thinking that this animal is any slouch. His peripheral vision has stymied the efforts of plenty, I mean plenty, of hunters before.

The one thing that allows him some leeway is he's so darn reproductive, he's made up for the number of times his brains have succumbed to a hunter's gun.

I've harvested my fair share of several types of bunnies. The funniest time was during a winter a couple of years ago in northwestern Utah. Christmas was over and I missed hunting badly, I really wanted some hunting action. But do you know how silly a grown woman looks, dressed to the hilt in down clothing, shotgun grasped ever ready in heavy gloved–hands, eyes at knee level looking for rabbit tracks in newly fallen snow?

My favorite stories of hunting cottontails are about the numbers of different animals and birds I manage to scare up. I've seen pheasants scurrying around laughing at me. I've seen deer who aren't frightened a bit of guns out-of-season. I've seen thousands and thousands of jackrabbits when I couldn't find a cottontail to save my soul. But I suspect I'm telling you tales you've already told yourself.

One warning I have to make: Be very careful when you handle rabbits, to avoid the possible infection of tularemia. I mention this only as a warning to the wise because everyone should feel comfortable with the fact that tularemia does not pose a problem to those eating the meat of rabbit if the meat is cooked well-done. I like to wear gloves when handling rabbits, just to make sure. But there are other ways you should be careful. For instance, San Stiver, the upland game specialist with the Nevada Department of Wildlife, told me about the time he contracted tularemia in his eye. He doesn't know how his eye was infected, but suspects a stray hair must have gotten in there. It's only smart to be as careful as you possibly can.

Because so many hunters hunt rabbits, there are a great number of ways to prepare them for the table. I wouldn't doubt that the most traditional way is a hasenpfeffer. Nearly everyone has his own answer to a hasenpfeffer and I would be remiss not to have included one in this book.

One recipe I've chosen to include is for Rabbit Cacciatore. I was surprised when I found a variation of this recipe used for chicken in an Italian cookbook. I thought *cacciatore* meant 'with tomatoes' because Chicken Cacciatore, in my mind, has tomatoes in it. Capice?

I was wrong because *cacciatore* means 'hunter's style'. I think you'll enjoy this particular recipe, even though there aren't any tomatoes in it. If you must have tomatoes with your cacciatore, I've included a recipe with tomatoes in it. You'll like them both, I'm sure of it.

HASENPFEFFER
Serves 4

1 or 2 rabbits, quartered
1 cup vinegar
1 cup water
6 peppercorns
1 teaspoon salt
½ cup sugar
1 bay leaf
2 stalks celery, sliced
2 carrots, sliced
1 onion, sliced
2 tablespoons flour
½ cup sour cream

Combine vinegar, water, peppercorns, salt, sugar, and bay leaf in flat dish large enough to hold the rabbit pieces and marinade. Add the rabbit pieces, stirring well. Marinade rabbit in refrigerator for 48 hours, turning several times.

Add sliced celery, carrot, and onion to rabbit mixture. Cover. Micro on high 7 minutes. Simmer 20 minutes on medium. Remove rabbit from mixture. Keep warm.

Pour marinade and vegetables into food processor or blender. Process until smooth (or strain through vegetable strainer). Stir in flour and sour cream. Micro gravy on high 2 minutes to heat. Arrange rabbit pieces on platter and pour gravy over the rabbit. Serve extra gravy with the rabbit.

RABBIT IN WHITE WINE
Serves 2

1 large rabbit or 2 small ones, cut in serving pieces
3 tablespoons butter
1 onion, sliced
1 carrot, sliced
2 stalks celery, diced
Salt and pepper, to taste
¼ teaspoon thyme
¼ teaspoon marjoram
1 cup chicken bouillon
2 tablespoons vinegar
½ cup dry white wine
¼ cup sour cream

In 2-quart casserole, microwave butter 1 minute on high to melt. Add onion, carrot, and celery. Stir well to coat. Micro on high 2 minutes.

In a separate bowl, combine salt and pepper, thyme, marjoram, bouillon, vinegar, and white wine. Mix thoroughly.

Place rabbit pieces on top of vegetable mixture in 2-quart casserole. Pour white wine/seasoning mixture over top of rabbit pieces and vegetables.

Cover. Micro on high 5 minutes. Micro on bake or 60 percent power setting for 7 minutes. Stir. Micro on bake 5 minutes more. Stir in sour cream. Micro on bake 5 minutes to complete.

Serve over buttered noodles or on a platter surrounded by fresh green vegetables such as broccoli.

RABBIT WITH CURRY SAUCE
Serves 4

   2 rabbits, quartered
     Flour
2–3 tablespoons olive oil
   4 tablespoons butter
   1 clove garlic, minced
   2 medium zucchini, chopped
   1 medium onion, chopped
   ½ teaspoon curry
   2 tablespoons flour
     Salt to taste
   1 cup chicken bouillon
2–3 cups cooked, buttered noodles

Dust rabbit with flour. Heat oil in heavy stovetop skillet; add the rabbit and brown on all sides.

In a 3-quart casserole, micro butter 1 minute on high. Add garlic and micro on high 2 minutes. Remove the garlic from the butter and discard. Add zucchini, onion, and curry. Micro on high for 4 minutes. Stir in 2 tablespoons flour. Add salt to taste. Add bouillon and stir well.

Add the rabbit pieces and cover tightly. Micro on high 3–5 minutes or until boiling. Reduce power to 60 percent and microwave for 15–18 minutes or until rabbit is cooked thoroughly. Turn the rabbit pieces and stir the sauce one or two times during the cooking time.

Allow to sit for 5 minutes before serving. Serve over buttered noodles.

RABBIT CACCIATORE
Serves 4

2 rabbits, quartered
Salt
Freshly ground pepper
¼ cup olive oil
½ medium onion, chopped
2 cloves garlic, minced
¼ cup dry white wine
2 tablespoons white vinegar
¼ cup chicken bouillon or broth
½ teaspoon dried oregano, crumbled
1 bay leaf
3 tablespoons black olives, slivered
1 tablespoon capers

Rinse the rabbit with cold water and pat dry. Season the pieces with a little salt and a few grindings of fresh black pepper.

Heat the olive oil in a heavy skillet and add the rabbit pieces. Brown on all sides.

Remove the rabbit to a plate. Pour the leftover oil in a 3-quart casserole (add a little more oil if necessary). Add onion and garlic and micro on high 4 minutes. Add the wine and vinegar and micro on high 5 minutes. Pour in chicken broth and micro on high 1 minute. Add the rabbit pieces, oregano, and bay leaf. Cover and micro on high 3–5 minutes or until sauce is boiling. Stir.

Reduce power to 50 percent or bake and micro for 15–18 minutes until rabbit is cooked through. Arrange the pieces on a platter and cover with foil shiny side down.

Stir black olives and capers into the sauce. Mix 2 tablespoons with a little of the hot sauce and then pour back into the rest of the sauce. Micro on high for 1 minute to thicken. Pour the sauce over the rabbit.

Note: This is a delicious dish. The flavor of the sauce is unique. You're probably surprised that there are no tomatoes in this recipe. An Italian term *alla cacciatora* translates to 'hunter's style'. I think this recipe is appropriately named and although there are no tomatoes, I'm sure you'll enjoy this dish.

RABBIT CACCIATORE TOO
Serves 2–3

1 rabbit, cut into serving pieces
3 tablespoons olive oil
2 cups whole tomatoes, canned or fresh, chopped
½ medium onion, chopped
1 clove garlic, minced
1 cup chicken bouillon
½ teaspoon oregano
¼ teaspoon rosemary
¼ teaspoon thyme

Rinse and pat the rabbit dry. Heat oil in a heavy skillet and brown the rabbit pieces on all sides.

Place the rabbit pieces in a glass baking dish large enough to hold them.

Mix the remaining ingredients and stir well. Pour the sauce over the rabbit. Cover well. Micro on high for 5 minutes. Reduce the power and micro on 50 percent or simmer for 15–18 minutes until the juices of the rabbit run clear. Remove from the oven and allow to sit for 3–5 minutes before serving.

MEXICAN RABBIT

Serves 2–3

1 rabbit, cut into serving pieces
4 tablespoons butter
1 clove garlic, minced
Salt, to taste
1 cup chicken bouillon
1 onion, chopped
1 green pepper, chopped
½ cup black olives, sliced
2 cups tomatoes, chopped
3 tablespoons flour
1 cup canned corn

In a heavy skillet, melt the butter and add the rabbit pieces and garlic. Brown the rabbit on all sides.

Pour the rabbit, butter, and garlic mixture in a glass baking dish. Add salt and chicken bouillon. Cover. Micro on high for 5 minutes. Reduce power to 50 percent or simmer and micro for 15–17 minutes until the rabbit is cooked through. Remove the meat from the bones and discard the bones. Save 1 cup of the cooking broth.

In 2-quart casserole or bowl mix the onion, pepper, olives, and tomatoes. Cover and micro on high for 5 minutes stirring once during the cooking time. With a whisk, stir in the flour. Pour in the cooking broth from the rabbit. Micro on 80 percent for 3–4 minutes or until the mixture is thickened.

In an 8-inch square baking dish, spoon the corn in an even layer. Place a layer of the rabbit meat on top of the corn. Add the tomato mixture on top of the rabbit meat.

Cover well and micro on 70 percent or roast for 5–8 minutes until heated through.

Squirrel

Many, many young hunters begin their long lifetime of hunting on squirrels. I began my hunting career on ground squirrels near my hometown of Elko, Nevada. Of course, this wasn't hunting in the true sense of the word and the ground squirrels were merely pests that made good moving targets. They rank right up there with jackrabbits in the pest category and also the abundance category in my home state.

It took me a few years to realize that I was missing out on something wonderful. There were parts of the country where big hardwood trees grow. In the hardwood trees are scurrying little creatures that are the same kind of quick target as ground squirrels, but to my amazement, you can eat those kind of squirrels. It always seemed such a shame to shoot those little ground squirrels and let them stay where they fell. But we were warned not to pick up the squirrels and I don't know of anyone who would actually eat them.

I finally discovered what I was missing with the bushytails. They are fun creatures, to watch and to feed. The little robber baron probably spends as much time in children's films as the cottontail rabbit or deer fawn. However, this wasn't the excitement that I really was missing.

I discovered what worthy targets they are. Squirreling is a fine way to introduce a hunter to the sport. While some people prefer shotguns on squirrels, the real challenge is taking them with a .22 caliber rifle that has a low power scope.

While the squirrels are not large targets, they are quick and evasive, and abundant in their habitat. The squirrels leap through the trees, scurrying in and out of sight. This is often frustrating to the beginning gunner, but when a hit is scored he feels a genuine sense of accomplishment.

Fox and gray squirrels make excellent vittles. This is really where I missed out while hunting the nasty, little ground squirrels. The flavor of tree squirrels is very good. If you've never tried them, you're really missing out on some fine fare.

It's best to cook squirrels in some sort of liquid. They can frequently be tough and a little dry if they're old animals and cooking them in liquid helps eliminate that possibility. Becasue this method works so well on squirrels, the microwave is a natural for cooking them.

BREADED BAKED SQUIRREL
Serves 4

3 squirrels, cut into pieces
½ cup bread crumbs
2 tablespoons cornmeal
¼ teaspoon dry mustard
1 tablespoon parsley flakes
¼ teaspoon dry chicken bouillon
½ teaspoon onion powder
Salt and pepper
Paprika
Hot Mustard Sauce (see p. 176)

Combine bread crumbs, cornmeal, dry mustard, parsley flakes, bouillon powder, onion powder, salt, and pepper in a bag. Add squirrel pieces. Shake to coat squirrel pieces.

Place squirrel pieces in an 8- or 9-inch square baking dish. (It will take two layers.)

Cover with plastic wrap. Micro on 70 percent power or roast setting for 20 minutes. Let sit covered for 5 minutes to finish cooking.

Sprinkle pieces with paprika. Serve with Hot Mustard Sauce for individual dipping.

SQUASH AND SQUIRRELS
Serves 4

2 squirrels, cut in pieces
3 tablespoons butter
½ medium onion, sliced
2 cups chicken bouillon
4 small crookneck squash (about 2½ cups), sliced

Roux:
½ cup butter
½ cup flour

Melt 3 tablespoons butter in frying pan. Add onions. Sauté on stove top until onions are transparent. Add squirrels, cook 3–4 minutes each side.

Pour squirrels and onions in 3-quart casserole. Add bouillon and squash. Cover. Micro on 70 percent power setting for 10 minutes.

Meanwhile make roux. Melt butter in heavy saucepan on stove. When butter is hot, add flour. Reduce heat. Cook until caramel colored, stirring constantly.

(Squirrels may be done by this time. Let sit while making roux.)

Remove squirrels from bouillon. Stir in roux. (Carefully! It's hot!) Stir until well combined. Add some more bouillon if too thick.

Return squirrels to mixture. Micro on 70 percent or roast setting for 10–12 minutes until juices of squirrel run clear.

Note: The roux won't work in the microwave since there's no direct heat to brown the mixture.

Mixed Bag

Any hunter who grew up with the "you shoot it, you eat it" philosophy has probably had to suffer through game meals of some pretty unsavory critters. While in the course of writing this cookbook, I met a few of these people who had game in their freezer they were only too glad to get rid of.

I know hunters who throw something they've slain in the freezer thinking they'll thaw it out and cook it for the next game feed they're invited to. Their wives dutifully give away what they can and trash what ends up hopelessly freezer burned.

My sister-in-law Joyce Kofron and her husband Dale are examples of this phenomenon. A couple of years ago during a turkey hunting trip to Missouri, Dale and his buddy knocked off hunting about noon, but decided to sharpen up their skills on the abundant ground hogs in the area. Two skinned ground hogs ended up in the Kofrons' freezer.

While my husband and I were visiting her home in Iowa, Joyce was kind enough to donate some squirrels to my cookbook cause. She came across the ground hogs while digging through the freezer.

She jokingly suggested I try cooking them. Silly me, I took her up on the offer. Well, one Missouri ground hog was freezer burned, so he didn't have the opportunity to travel west in my cooler to succumb to the microwaves in my oven. Lucky him.

The other poor guy did. Well, I couldn't find a recipe for ground hogs, so I devised a new one and I got busy with this little critter. You know, he wasn't that bad.

The meat was a little hard to get at because of the tough tendons and other connective tissues, but with a little picking with teeth and fingers, I got enough to make a meal.

Anyway, if you or any other hunter in your household ever brings home a ground hog, you'll know what to do with him. In the meantime, this recipe would be very good on squirrels, rabbits, or doves.

Jim Zumbo, the author of the foreword to this book and good friend of mine, told me he'd had a raccoon in the freezer for over a year. If I could make something delectable out of that old piece of hide, I was a certified genius in the kitchen in his eyes.

First of all, I smelled the raccoon and he didn't smell all that taste tempting, but I did have to admit that he had more meat on him than that old ground hog did. So I decided to marinade the critter. I marinaded him overnight, then developed a stew of sorts.

After I played with the cooking times, he finally was cooked and I took him out of the oven. The meat was juicy, it wasn't tough. But I'll tell you, I wouldn't go out of my way to eat raccoon again. Neither would my father, who refused to swallow the meat. My golden retriever carried around a thigh for a week not wanting to lose it, but not committing herself to eating it, either.

Now I know some people find raccoon a culinary delight; I'm just not one of them. But in case you like the taste of raccoon, I've included the recipe for it here.

I've included recipes for wild boar here for lack of a better section in which to place them. Many hunters in Nevada travel to northern California where the hunting on boars is excellent.

John and Kristin Lee of Reno, Nevada introduced me to wild boar. John shot one while hunting California. The meat was excellent. Of course, with wild boar, you should make certain the meat is well cooked to eliminate the possibility of trichinosis. If you have a large, old boar, you might parboil the meat before you follow any of the recipes here. That will help tenderize the meat.

So now you know what the meaning of "mixed bag" is. This section is for all those game animals that sacrificed themselves to my microwave and don't have a section to call their own.

BURGUNDY CREAM GROUND HOG
Serves 2–3

*1 medium-sized ground hog, cut into pieces
(or 3 squirrels or 6 doves or 2 rabbits)*

All-purpose Game Marinade: *(See recipe p. 179)*
*½ cup flour, approximately
7 tablespoons butter
¾ cup hearty Burgundy wine
1½ cups beef bouillon or broth
½ cups onion, chopped
2 cups mushrooms, sliced
1 cup sour cream
Buttered noodles
Parsley*

Add pieces of ground hog to marinade. Cover. Refrigerate for 48 hours, turning occasionally.

Remove ground hog from marinade. Drain and pat dry with toweling.

Coat pieces with flour. Brown in 3 tablespoons melted butter, either using conventional method in a saucepan on stovetop or using manufacturer's directions on a microwave browning dish. Place browned pieces in a 3-quart casserole.

Mix ½ cup wine with 1½ cups beef bouillon.

Micro 2 tablespoons butter 1 minute on high in small saucepan. Add onions. Micro on high 2 minutes. Add to wine mixture.

Pour wine mixture over ground hog pieces. Cover. Micro on high 5 minutes. Micro on 50 percent or simmer for 15 minutes. Turn once. Let sit while preparing mushrooms.

Micro 2 tablespoons butter in microproof saucepan for 1 minute on high to melt. Add mushrooms. Micro on high 3 minutes.

Drain ground hog pieces, reserving 1 cup liquid. Place ground hog pieces on serving dish lined with buttered noodles.

Combine reserved cooking liquid with 1 cup sour cream, mushrooms, and ¼ cup Burgundy wine. Pour over ground hog pieces.

Garnish with parsley.

Note: Serve plenty of napkins with this one. It's messy, but you'll want to use your fingers and teeth to reach the tasty, little, red meat morsels.

STEWED UP RACCOON
Serves 5–6

1 raccoon, cut into serving pieces
2–3 tablespoons salt
½ cup white vinegar
1 onion, quartered
2 carrots, cut in chunks
2 cups beef broth or bouillon
12 peppercorns

In a large bowl, mix raccoon, water to cover, salt, and vinegar. Marinade overnight.

Place raccoon pieces in the bottom of a 2-quart casserole. Place the separated onion pieces and carrots on top of the meat. Pour the beef broth or bouillon over the meat and vegetables. Sprinkle the peppercorns over the mixture.

Cover tightly. Microwave on 50 percent or simmer for 25 minutes. Allow to sit for 5 minutes before serving.

Note: The raccoon I cooked in this manner came out just fine. The meat was tender and juicy. I, personally, don't care for the flavor of raccoon, as much as I hate to break it to you. For those of you who enjoy the flavor of the red meat, you'll enjoy this recipe.

PEPPERY RACCOON
Serves 5–6

1 raccoon, cut into serving pieces
1 cup oil
1 cup white vinegar
2 cloves garlic, sliced
2–3 tablespoons coarsely ground pepper
Salt, to taste
1 onion, sliced
¼ cup water

Place raccoon in a glass bowl large enough to hold the meat. Mix oil, vinegar, and garlic together and pour over the meat. Marinade overnight, stirring every once in a while to coat.

Drain pieces. Pat dry with toweling. Roll pieces in ground pepper to coat. Place the coated pieces in a 2-quart casserole. Sprinkle with salt, if desired. Arrange the onion slices over the meat pieces. Add ¼ cup water to the casserole. Cover tightly.

Microwave on 50 percent or simmer setting for 25–30 minutes or until the meat close to the bones is free from red juices.

Note: I didn't like the raccoon cooked in this recipe any better, although the pepper does mask the gamey flavor somewhat. I guess I'll never be a big fan of the critters.

BAKED WILD BOAR CHOPS
Serves 2–4

4 boar chops
3–4 tablespoons oil
½ cup maple syrup
4 tablespoons catsup
1 teaspoon dried mustard
1 teaspoon cider vinegar
Cornstarch (optional)

Cut the excess fat off the chops. Heat the oil in a heavy skillet and brown the chops quickly. Place the chops in a glass baking dish.

Mix the maple syrup, catsup, mustard, and vinegar in a small bowl. Stir until the mustard is dissolved. Pour the sauce over the chops.

Micro on 70 percent or roast for 8–10 minutes until the juices run clear. (Wild boar should be cooked thoroughly.) Remove from oven and cover with aluminum foil for 3–5 minutes before serving.

Thicken the sauce with cornstarch, if desired. Spoon the sauce over the chops.

LEG OF WILD BOAR
Serves 6–8

1 wild boar leg
2 cloves garlic, slivered
1 tablespoon fennel seeds
3 tablespoons oil
2 teaspoons poultry seasoning
Freshly ground black pepper
Flour (optional)

Cut the excess fat off the leg. Cut thin slits in the roast all over the top, sides, and bottom. Insert a sliver of garlic and a few fennel seeds in each slit.

Heat the oil in a heavy skillet. Brown the outside of the roast on all sides.

Place the roast in a baking dish large enough to hold it. Sprinkle the remaining fennel seeds over the outside of the roast. Dust with poultry seasoning. Grind black pepper liberally over the roast.

Insert temperature probe or microproof meat thermometer in the thickest part of the roast, making sure not to touch the bone. Cover loosely with plastic wrap. Micro at 60 percent or bake until the temperature reaches 165 degrees. Turn over the roast halfway through the cooking time to ensure even cooking. Wild boar should be cooked thoroughly to avoid the threat of trichinosis.

Remove from oven and cover with foil, shiny side down, to finish cooking.

Serve with the pan drippings. (Thicken the pan drippings with flour, if you wish. Make certain to drain off most of the fat.)

Big Game

Antelope

    Antelope are the most underrated big game animals that roam the face of the earth. They just get no respect at all. There is a common and widespread notion that antelope meat is everything from strong and gamey to absolutely inedible. I don't know about these claims, because I've eaten a lot of antelope meat and I've found it to be neither strong nor gamey. In fact, antelope is one of my favorite game meats and has certainly earned my respect.

    Of course, there are several common denominators present when a meal of pleasant-tasting antelope is served. The most important thing to understand is how important care is when hunting, field dressing, transporting, and butchering antelope. Special techniques are necessary to assure a palatable cut of meat.

If the reasons behind these techniques are not known, it's difficult to understand why they are so important.

First of all, most antelope are shot when weather conditions are extremely warm. If the meat does not receive immediate care under these conditions, the spoiling process begins as soon as the meat's down. The first thing you need to do is to field dress your animal using normal precaution. The next step, which is actually the most important one, is to get the skin off the animal just as quickly as possible. When skinning the antelope, make sure none of the antelope hair touches the meat. Hang your antelope in a cool, dry place, covered with a game bag, until it can be taken to the processor or until you process it yourself.

During the warm months of late summer and early fall when most antelope are shot, this process can be near to impossible. But the better care you take of your animal, the better it will taste. Antelope don't need the aging process that deer do, so they can be processed immediately.

Unfortunately, those who can't stand the taste of antelope usually hunt when it's warm outside, pop their buck a hundred miles from their processor, field dress him hastily, throw him in the back of their truck where he's coated by road dirt and dust or, worse yet, toss him in the trunk of their car. Under these circumstances, it's no wonder their animal tastes bad.

There are other circumstances that ruin the flavor of the meat. Most shots made on antelope are long shots at standing antelope. Running shots aren't easy ones to make and shooting an animal who's pumped up with adrenaline probably doesn't provide the best eating either. I made a "Hail Mary" shot on an antelope running hell bent for leather during my 1983 Nevada antelope hunt. He was a beautiful 15½-inch buck and I couldn't resist trying to bring him down when my first long shot failed.

He tasted great, but I think the reason was because we handled the meat so carefully. It wasn't that warm when I shot him, it was early in the cool Nevada morning. We took care of him properly, too.

The cooking method you use will also have a good deal to do with how your antelope tastes. The microwave is a good way to cook certain cuts of meat and certain recipes of antelope. The one thing you'll want to avoid is overcooking the meat. The first time I cooked antelope chops in the microwave, I figured I'd cook them about the time I would cook pork chops of the same thickness. They were about as tasty and chewy as a cardboard box. They were cooked about three times as long as necessary.

My greatest compliment on my antelope cooking talents came when I cooked one of the recipes in this section for my father for dinner. He told me it was some of the most tender *beef* he had ever tasted. He raised his eyebrows when I told him it wasn't beef.

Antelope are not easy game to pursue, they just appear that way because they are plentiful. They provide excellent long-range challenges for the hunter and will hone stalking skills as well. They are cautious, wily creatures and they can run like the dickens. They deserve a place of honor among their other big game companions. If you're conscientious about their field care, you'll also have an epicurean delight.

ANTELOPE CHOPS
Serves 4

8 antelope chops
¼ pound mushrooms, sliced
1 clove garlic, minced
2 tablespoons oil
6 tablespoons butter
½ onion, chopped finely

Gravy:
3 tablespoons fat
4 tablespoons flour
2 cups hot water
1 teaspoon Kitchen Bouquet gravy flavoring

Microwave mushrooms and garlic in oil on high for 3 minutes. Set aside. In large casserole dish, micro the butter on high for 1 minute. Stir in onions. Micro on high 1 minute. Place chops in casserole. Cover. Micro on high 4 minutes. Turn chops over. Recover. Micro on high 4 minutes more.

Remove chops and onions from fat. Save 3 tablespoons fat for gravy. Return the 3 tablespoons to casserole. Stir in 4 tablespoons flour. Add 2 cups hot water. Stir well. Micro on high until desired thickness, stirring every couple of minutes until cooking time is complete (approximately 6–8 minutes). Stir in Kitchen Bouquet and mushrooms. Micro on high 1 minute. Serve gravy over chops.

SWEET AND SOUR ANTELOPE
Serves 6

    1 *pound antelope round steak, cut into thin strips, approximately ½ inch wide*
1¾ *cups water*
    1 *teaspoon salt*
 ¼ *cup soy sauce*
    1 *clove garlic*
 ⅓ *cup sugar*
 ¼ *cup cornstarch*
 ¼ *cup cider vinegar*
 ⅓ *cup pineapple juice*
 ¼ *teaspoon ginger*
 ¾ *cup pineapple chunks*
    1 *bell pepper, cut in 1-inch chunks*
      Sesame seeds
      Rice

Place antelope strips, water, salt, soy sauce, and garlic in a 2-quart saucepan. Cook on high until at a boil, approximately 5 minutes. Cover. Cook on simmer or medium until meat is just barely cooked, about 12–15 minutes. Discard garlic. Drain the broth through coffee filter or cheesecloth to remove meat drippings. Set meat aside. Reserve broth.

In a saucepan, blend the sugar, cornstarch, vinegar, pineapple juice, and ginger until smooth. Gradually stir in meat broth. Cook on high until sauce is thick and transparent, stopping and stirring every two minutes until done, approximately 6–8 minutes.

Combine the sauce with antelope slices, pineapple chunks, sesame seeds, and bell pepper. Let sit for several minutes, covered, to finish cooking. Stir. Serve over bed of rice.

ANTELOPE KABOBS
Serves 4

½ *pound antelope round steak,*
  cut in 1-inch cubes

Marinade:
⅓ *cup Worcestershire sauce*
½ *cup oil*
¼ *cup white vinegar*
½ *teaspoon onion powder*
¼ *teaspoon oregano*

1 *bell pepper, cut in 1-inch cubes*
8 *cherry tomatoes*
4 *small boiling onions, quartered*
8 *wooden shish kabob skewers*
  Rice

Mix the ingredients for the marinade together in shallow dish. Add round steak cubes. Marinade in refrigerator for at least 3 hours.

Starting with piece of pepper, alternate vegetables with pieces of antelope meat on wooden skewer. Brush vegetables with remaining marinade.

Place kabobs on a bacon rack. (If you don't have a bacon rack, use a bowl, placing the edges of the skewers on the sides of the bowl so the vegetables and meat pieces are suspended over the bowl.) Cover lightly with plastic wrap. Micro on roast or 70 percent power setting for 8 minutes. Make sure the meat is not overcooked.

Serve over bed of rice.

Note: It's best to use slightly underripe tomatoes in the microwave since they tend to overcook quickly. I place the cherry tomatoes in the center of the kabob to prevent overcooking, since the microwave cooks food on the outside edges quickly.

GARDEN FRESH GUMBO
Serves 8–10

2 pounds antelope round steak or stew meat,
  cut into bite-sized pieces

Roux:
1 cup butter
1 cup flour

1 onion, chopped
3 tablespoons oil
2 stalks celery, chopped
3 carrots, chopped
1 zucchini, chopped
3 sprigs parsley, chopped
1 clove garlic, chopped
1 cup corn
1 cup cut string beans
2 cups water
1 48-ounce can tomato juice
  Salt and pepper, to taste

To make roux: Melt 1 cup butter in heavy saucepan on stove. Stir in flour. Heat until boiling. Reduce heat. Stir constantly until dark brown. Don't overbrown or overcook. (*Note:* This method will not work in a microwave oven since the microwave will not allow the browning process to occur.) Set aside.

Cook meat and onion with oil in medium microproof saucepan 5 minutes on high. Drain.

Combine meat, onion, celery, carrots, zucchini, parsley, garlic, corn, string beans, water, juice, salt, and pepper, in very large bowl (or split into 2 large saucepans or bowls). Stir the roux into ingredients, stirring constantly so roux blends completely.

Cook on high 5 minutes. Stir. Cook on simmer for 25–30 minutes. Serve steaming with sourdough bread.

Note: I usually take half this recipe and freeze it for a later date before the final cooking stage. Then when you're ready to use the gumbo, defrost and heat it in the same freezing container. Make sure your freezing container is microproof.

SAUCY BARBECUED CHOPS
Serves 4

8 antelope chops

Sauce:
1 tablespoon chopped onion
1 tablespoon oil
½ clove garlic
1 6-ounce can tomato paste
⅔ cup water
¼ teaspoon chili powder
1 teaspoon Worcestershire sauce
2 tablespoons vinegar
1 tablespoon Dijon mustard
2 tablespoons catsup

Place onion, oil, and garlic in microproof saucepan. Micro on high 2 minutes. Add remaining ingredients. Stir thoroughly.

Place chops in a single layer in glass baking dish. Pour sauce over the top of the chops.

Micro on high 2 minutes, then reduce power to roast or 60 percent setting for 12–13 minutes. Remove from microwave and cover with foil shiny side down for 3 minutes to finish cooking.

FAST ANTELOPE STEAKS
Serves 4

2 pounds antelope steak, thinly sliced and pounded
2 tablespoons butter
1 clove garlic, minced
1 teaspoon fresh parsley, minced
¼ teaspoon onion powder
1 bunch green onions, sliced

Melt butter on high 1 minute in microwave. Add remaining ingredients, except steaks, to butter. Pour into large baking dish.

Add steaks. Cover. Microwave 6 minutes on sauté or 90 percent power setting, turning once.

Cover with aluminum foil, shiny side down, to finish cooking.

JAY DAHL'S CURRIED ANTELOPE
Serves 6

2 pounds antelope steak, cut in cubes
1 medium onion, chopped
2 tablespoons bacon fat
1 cup beef bouillon
1 tablespoon curry powder
2 tablespoons catsup
1 teaspoon A-1 sauce
2 teaspoons Worcestershire sauce
1 teaspoon lemon juice
¼ teaspoon turmeric
¼ cup margarine
1 cup sour cream
1 cup canned mushrooms
   Spinach noodles, buttered

In a 3-quart casserole, sauté onion in bacon fat by microwaving on high for 3 minutes. Add meat and microwave 6–7 minutes, stirring several times, until the meat is browned on all sides.

Add other ingredients except sour cream, mushrooms, and noodles. Cover loosely. Micro on high for 5 minutes. Stir. Reduce power to 50 percent or simmer and cook 20–25 minutes until meat is tender.

Stir in sour cream and mushrooms and micro on 50 percent for 2 minutes to heat sour cream. Remove from microwave and cover with foil for 5 minutes. Serve over warm, buttered spinach noodles.

Note: This is delicious.

STUFFED ANTELOPE CHOPS
Serves 4

8 thin antelope chops
2 tablespoons oil
3 tablespoons butter, melted
1 cup cornbread stuffing
3 tablespoons raisins
3 tablespoons chopped apricots
1 tablespoon chopped pecans
¼ teaspoon sage
¼ teaspoon thyme
¼ cup milk
   Applesauce

Trim all the fat from the chops, if not already done. Heat the oil in a heavy skillet and brown the chops quickly on both sides. Place four of the chops in an 8-inch square baking dish.

In medium bowl, mix remaining ingredients, except applesauce, stir well. Divide stuffing in four parts and mound the stuffing on top of each of the four chops in the baking dish.

Place the remaining chops on top of each of the four in the dish. Cover tightly. Micro on 70 percent or roast for 8–12 minutes until the bottom chops are cooked. Turn the dish a quarter turn once during the cooking time.

Serve with applesauce.

Deer

Venison is probably the most widely consumed of any big game meat. Deer are widely dispersed over most of the United States. Most young hunters begin their introduction to big game hunting with an annual traditional deer hunt. That tradition is carried on for many, many years.

Venison, or any big game for that matter, requires initial care in the field long before the meat ever makes it to your kitchen. The animal's forage food has a great deal to do with how the meat will taste, but I'm still convinced that any game meat can be turned into a culinary delight depending on how it's cared for in the field.

My father always remarks how good the venison I serve is, chalking it up to good field care. I must stress the importance of conscientious game care. There are many books out on the subject of field care as it applies to the finished product—the dinner on your table. My favorite was done by my good friend Sam Fadala. *Game Care and Cookery* is a must for any game cook.

Besides the care that is given to downed meat when properly field dressing it, transporting it, aging and butchering it, care must be given to make the best possible shot on your animal. A shot on a highly stressed animal that is full of adrenaline or a poor shot that only wounds your animal are a few examples of the thought you must give to the shot you'll take if you want premium meat.

I won't go into the specifics on caring for your game in the field or butchering or any of the other how-to's of game meat preparation. But I will stress that "you can't make a silk purse out of a sow's ear." If your initial product is not good, nothing you do in the microwave will change that.

The microwave is excellent for cooking game meat. The one thing you must make sure of is not to overcook the meat. Anyone who has had less than satisfactory results with game in the microwave was probably cooking the meat too fast at too high a power setting. I've heard all kinds of comments, mostly negative, about cooking game in a microwave. I've had excellent results with it is the only answer I can give. It works.

The recipes I've included in any of the big game sections here can be interchanged. For instance, an elk roast recipe would also work well on a venison roast as long as the roasts are close to the same size. The recipes I wrote in this deer section were put here for a reason—I tested the recipe with that kind of meat, so I can assure good results using that specific cut of that specific kind of game.

Some people disfavor venison because of its gamey taste. I've tasted gamey meat before, too. Luckily it wasn't shot by me. But some of the recipes in this cookbook are a little heavier on the seasonings or on the sauces to help mask the gamey flavor of some meat. Choose those recipes that are heavy-handed with spices if you have a below par piece of meat to prepare.

When you set out the meat before cooking it, check the meat to make sure all the fat is cut out of the meat. If it isn't, you'll want to trim away as much of the fat as you can because the fat often contains some strong flavors.

I once thought roasting methods of cooking would not work in the microwave, so I avoided roast recipes like the plague. I finally decided to try roasting meat in the microwave. The big game I tried was excellent, without question. I was truly surprised. The only prerequisite was to cook the meat at a low setting for a longer period of time.

I have not found a problem with the fact that the microwave does not brown meat. Most game meat is red meat anyway and I'm not picky about there being no brown on top. I would have a problem with eating unbrowned pork chops, but unbrowned venison steaks don't bother me.

In some of the recipes, I recommend browning the meat in a stovetop skillet or a microwave browning dish before adding the rest of the ingredients. Often this is not done for cosmetic purposes, but to seal in the juices. I don't like the microwave browning dishes I've seen. Often they're just too small to do a job quickly and they're often miserable to clean. If you want to use them that's great and I certainly would encourage you to do so. I am not a microwave oven purist, so I'll use a quick, hot skillet for the job.

I've used recipes for a number of different cuts of meat here. There are tastes to suit almost anyone. I'm sure you'll find a few new favorites here among those I've included.

You don't need special recipes for your venison. In many instances you can use this meat instead of beef in recipes. When I first went to college, I made some friends in Reno whom I admired a lot. Nearly their entire diet of meat consisted of venison. It was an annual tradition for their family to go deer hunting and both husband and wife eagerly looked forward to it. When their children came along, they hauled the kids with them.

She made excellent soups and hearty stews. Her spaghetti sauce was pretty good, especially since she wasn't Italian. I was jealous that I had to eat dorm food. I didn't hide my joy too much when I was invited to dinner.

I didn't know that within a decade after that, my menus would consist largely of game meat, especially venison. I rarely eat anything but fish and game anymore and I don't miss the beef at all. Whenever I eat out at a restaurant, I order fare I can't obtain readily elsewhere—such as clams, mussels and calamari.

I'll trade you prime rib of beef for a venison steak anyday.

VENISON PEPPERS
Serves 4

1 pound ground venison
4 medium size green peppers
1 onion, chopped
1 teaspoon sage
1 clove garlic, minced
1 tablespoon soy sauce
1½ cups cooked rice
1 cup tomato sauce

Cut the tops off peppers. Remove the seeds and rinse them thoroughly. Place peppers in a shallow microproof dish. Add enough water to cover bottom of dish.

Cover. Micro on high 2 minutes. Allow peppers to sit covered while you prepare filling.

Filling: In medium microproof dish, combine chopped onion and crumbled ground meat. Micro on high 4 minutes or until meat is cooked, stirring once or twice to break up meat. Add sage, garlic, soy sauce, rice, and tomato sauce. Fill peppers, packing well.

Place stuffed peppers in microproof casserole dish. Add 2 tablespoons of water to the bottom of the dish. Cover well. Micro on high 8–10 minutes or until the peppers are tender. Allow to sit 2–3 minutes, covered, before serving to finish cooking.

TERRIFIC TERIYAKI
Serves 6

2 pounds venison round steak, cut into thin strips about 2 inches long
2 teaspoons powdered ginger
2 cloves garlic, minced
1 medium onion, chopped finely
2 tablespoons sugar
1 cup soy sauce
¼ cup hearty Burgundy wine
½ pound mushroom caps
   Wooden skewers
   Teriyaki sauce
   Rice

Combine ginger, garlic, onion, sugar, soy sauce, and wine. Add meat and mushrooms. Stir well. Let stand 2 hours, stirring occasionally.

Thread meat on skewers alternating with mushrooms. Brush with teriyaki sauce. Place on bacon rack or suspend over microproof bowl or dish.

Micro on high 8 minutes, turning once. Serve on a bed of rice.

PEPPER STEAK

Serves 4

1–1½ pounds venison round steak, cut in strips
¾ cup tomato juice
1 bell pepper, cut in strips
1 red bell pepper, cut in strips
1 onion, sliced
2 teaspoons cornstarch
2 tablespoons soy sauce
White rice

Preheat browning dish on high 7 minutes. Brown venison strips on both sides (or brown in frying pan on stovetop). Drain.

Combine steak, tomato juice, peppers, and onion in a 2-quart casserole. Mix cornstarch in soy sauce. Add to meat mixture. Cover. Micro on high 8 minutes.

Let stand, covered, 5 minutes before serving. Serve over a bed of rice.

TACO SALAD

Serves 8–10

1 pound ground venison
1 small package taco seasoning
1 head lettuce, cut in strips
2 cups mild cheddar cheese, shredded
½ cup pitted black olives, sliced
2 tomatoes, cut in small chunks
½ medium onion, chopped
1–1½ cups Thousand Island dressing
8 ounces taco-flavored tortilla chips

In microproof casserole, microwave ground venison on 90 percent until cooked, stirring to break up pieces every minute or so, about 6–7 minutes.

Add taco seasoning to ground venison. Drain and refrigerate meat until thoroughly chilled.

In large bowl mix venison, lettuce, cheddar cheese, olives, tomatoes, and onions. Add dressing and chips and toss well to coat. Add more dressing if necessary to coat all ingredients without soaking the chips.

Note: I am asked to make this salad at every occasion a potluck is called for. I used to make the recipe with beef but it honestly tastes better with venison. No one will call me on that one.

KIELBASA SANDWICHES
Serves 4

4 kielbasa sausages made with venison (or elk or antelope), slit about ¼ inch through the sausage lengthwise
1 green pepper, sliced
½ medium onion, chopped
1 teaspoon bacon fat
4 hard rolls, toasted

In microwave casserole, place sausages in single layer. Cover tightly. Micro on high 4 minutes.

Add green pepper, onion, and bacon fat. Cover. Micro on high 4 minutes or until vegetables are softened.

Spoon mixture on top of hard rolls to serve.

VENISON SKILLET DINNER
Serves 4–5

1 pound ground venison
1 cup mushrooms, sliced
2 cups beef bouillon
1 cup elbow macaroni
1 cup sour cream

In a large casserole, microwave ground venison for 6–7 minutes, stirring several times to cook evenly and break up pieces.

Add mushrooms, bouillon, and macaroni. Stir well. Cover tightly. Micro on 60 percent for 15 minutes or until macaroni is tender. (The cooking time can be reduced if the macaroni is cooked before adding.)

Remove from the oven and stir in sour cream.

VENISON STEW
Serves 4–6

2 pounds venison stew meat, cut in small cubes

Marinade:
1–1½ cups Burgundy wine
1 cup beef bouillon
2 tablespoons oil
12 peppercorns
2 garlic cloves, minced
A few grindings fresh pepper

Flour
Bacon fat
3 carrots, sliced
3 small zucchini, chopped
2 potatoes, cut in chunks
4 fresh medium tomatoes, quartered

Mix venison with wine, bouillon, oil, peppercorns, garlic, and pepper. Cover and refrigerate at least 4 hours. Drain the venison but reserve the marinade.

Dust the venison with flour and brown in bacon fat in either stovetop skillet or microwave browning dish.

Place the cubes in 3-quart bowl or casserole dish. Add remaining ingredients and reserved marinade. Cover.

Micro on high 3–5 minutes or until boiling. Reduce to 50 percent or simmer and cook for 30 minutes.

EASY VENISON RAGOUT
Serves 4

1 pound venison stew meat, cut in 1-inch cubes
1 package brown gravy mix
2 tablespoons flour
Freshly ground pepper, to taste
1 clove garlic, minced
1 teaspoon Worcestershire sauce
¼ cup Burgundy wine
2 carrots, sliced
2 stalks celery, sliced
2 potatoes, peeled and cubed
1 cup frozen peas, thawed and drained
1 cup beef broth

Lightly brown the venison in browning dish or skillet. Remove meat to 3-quart casserole. Add gravy mix. Stir well.

Add remaining ingredients. Stir well. Cook on 50 percent for 35 minutes or until meat and vegetables are tender. Stir occasionally during cooking time. Let stand 3–4 minutes before serving.

BURGUNDY VENISON STEW
Serves 4–5

1–1½ pounds venison stew meat, cut in 1-inch cubes
1 medium onion, sliced
1 cup hearty Burgundy wine
Flour
7 tablespoons butter
1 medium potato, cut in small cubes
2 carrots, chopped
3 stalks celery, chopped
1 bay leaf

Pour the venison and onions in a glass or plastic bowl and pour wine over them. Refrigerate 4–5 hours. Drain meat, but reserve wine and onions. Flour meat cubes. Melt 4 tablespoons of the butter in heavy, large stovetop skillet. Brown venison in butter, stirring continuously.

When the meat is brown, melt the rest of the butter in the skillet. Add potatoes, carrots, celery, and bay leaf, stirring continuously for 5–6 minutes (until everything gets really mushy).

Remove from stove and pour mixture into large bowl or casserole. Add a little of the wine to the frying pan to loosen up remaining particles stuck on the skillet bottom. Pour this and the reserved wine into the bowl with the rest of the stew. Add the onions as well. Stir well. Cover lightly.

Micro on 50 percent for 30 minutes or until potatoes are cooked through. Remove the bay leaf and serve steaming with thick slices of warm bread.

Elk

If I had to choose my favorite big game meat, it would have to be elk—hands down. I hate to make the choice because there are so many fine game meats to choose from. The first time I tasted elk it was mixed in a hearty tomato-based stew served by some of my friends in Oregon. They regularly hunted for elk and presented fine meals from their well-cared-for game.

Since elk are grazing animals, eating grasses instead of browse as deer do, their meat usually does not have that gamey taste associated with venison. Of course, elk should still be handled with the utmost of care in the field to assure the best possible pieces of meat to fill your freezer.

Most elk can be cooked as you would cook venison and of course when you're microwaving, the biggest caution is not to overcook the meat for the best possible results. In most of the big game recipes I've included, I usually specify how well the meat will be cooked giving the time frame I've suggested. Normally I recommend meat that is still a little pink on the inside. I have never been one to recommend game meat be well-done before it is edible.

Some game cooks are afraid that because the meat is wild it must be overcooked. There is no logical reason for this. Some microwave ovens have "hot spots" where the meat will cook better while other spots won't reach optimum internal temperatures. I have not had a problem with this in my microwave. If you notice your microwave oven "hot spotting," turning the dish a quarter turn one or two times during cooking will often cure the problem.

The only time this is of real concern is when cooking bear meat or pork, since the meat of these critters must be cooked thoroughly to avoid trichinosis. However, I've avoided this problem in this book because I haven't included any bear recipes. I've never taken a bear in an area where the meat is good to eat. The black bear I harvested several years ago was shot in a part of the country where the bears' main course is carrion. So, not only have I never experimented with cooking bear in any kind of oven, I've never tasted bear meat, although I've heard it is excellent. Be careful to cook the pork recipes well, too.

Elk steaks and elk roasts, as well as elk burger, are my favorite cuts of elk and all three cuts are excellent when cooked in the microwave. I was hesitant to cook either steaks or roasts in the microwave at first. I pulled a package of elk meat out of the freezer thinking it was a roast. I figured I'd try it and see if what everyone else was saying about cooking roasts in the microwave was true.

I normally like to quick fry or broil steaks, so I was dismayed at first when I saw four elk steaks facing me instead of a roast. I decided to try to cook the steaks as I would a roast with a temperature probe. The results were excellent. The meat was tender and moist. You'll find the recipe in this section. The results were so good, I tried cooking roasts in the microwave. I've had good results with all the meat I've tried microwaving.

I was a little intimidated by the microwave at first and was hesitant to use it on anything. Like my food processor, it sat virtually unused for anything but heating coffee or cooking hot dogs for the longest time. My food processor sat alongside the microwave because I thought it would take me longer to figure out how to use it than it would take to get out the chopping board and do it by hand.

Once I started using the microwave, I lost my apprehensions. It wasn't going to blow up. It wasn't going to bite me. No one was going to put the cat in it. It took a little bit of time, but I worked through a number of recipes and they came out just fine. I was thrilled to have such a help in my kitchen.

The hardest part of practicing with game meat is you can't go down to the grocery store and pick up another elk roast if you don't like the results of the microwave. Game meat is hard and expensive to come by. Especially if you've shot the game yourself, it's hard to turn it over to a machine you don't understand.

If you haven't taken the game yourself, it might be even harder. I can't imagine ruining a piece of game meat my husband has been beaming with pride over.

Cooking game meat has been reduced to the mystery level anyway. Most women I know are scared to death of cooking game. Many don't like game meat and will only use the meat when prodded by their husbands.

Cooking game in the microwave is easy. I hope I've included enough tips here to eliminate the questions. You'll be able to serve elk or any other wild animal, bird, or fish without hesitation.

THREE BEAN ELK CHILI
Serves 6–8

1 pound ground elk
1 green pepper, diced
1 onion, diced
2 cloves garlic, minced
1 28-ounce can whole tomatoes
1 15-ounce can pinto beans
1 15-ounce can kidney beans
1 15-ounce can black-eyed peas
1 teaspoon salt
1 teaspoon freshly ground pepper
3 tablespoons chili powder
¼ teaspooon cayenne pepper
1 teaspoon cumin

Combine elk meat, pepper, onion, and garlic in medium microproof saucepan. Micro on high 4 minutes. Stir to break up the meat. Micro on high 2 minutes more. Stir.

In 4-quart microproof casserole or bowl, combine meat mixture and the remaining ingredients. Adjust seasonings to taste.

Cover well. Micro on high 5 minutes or until boiling. Micro on simmer or 50 percent power setting 25–30 minutes. Let sit 4–5 minutes to continue cooking before serving.

Note: Canned beans provide better results when cooked in a microwave than cooked dried beans do.

FANTASTIC ELK STROGANOFF
Serves 8–10

  2 *pounds elk round steak, cut in thin strips 2 inches long*
  1 *cup butter*
1½ *cups onions, finely chopped*
1½ *pounds fresh mushrooms, sliced*
  6 *tablespoons flour*
  2 *cups beef broth or bouillon (2 bouillon cubes dissolved in 2 cups boiling water)*
1½ *teaspoons salt*
  6 *tablespoons tomato paste*
  2 *teaspoons Worcestershire sauce*
  ¾ *cup sour cream*
  1 *cup heavy cream*
  8 *cups cooked rice or cooked, wide, flat noodles*

Micro ⅓ cup butter in small saucepan 1 minute on high. Add onions and sauté on high 2 minutes. Set aside.

Micro ⅓ cup more of the butter in small saucepan 1 minute on high. Add mushrooms and sauté on high 2 minutes. Set aside.

Melt remaining butter in large saucepan or casserole. Add meat. Micro on high 3 minutes. Stir. Micro on high 3 minutes more. Stir. Micro on high 3 minutes more. Stir. (Total cooking time of 9 minutes). Add the flour. Stir well.

Add bouillon, salt, and onions. Cover. Micro on high 5 minutes. Micro on simmer or 50 percent power 12–15 minutes until meat is just barely cooked through.

Add tomato paste, Worcestershire sauce, sour cream, heavy cream, and the mushrooms.

Micro on high 3–4 minutes to heat thoroughly.

Serve stroganoff over rice or noodles.

ELK SIRLOIN STEAKS

Serves 4

4 sirloin-cut elk steaks, about 8 ounces each
3 tablespoons soy sauce
2 tablespoons steak sauce
¼ onion, coarsely chopped
¼ teaspoon ground pepper
2 stalks celery, sliced

In a small bowl, mix soy sauce, steak sauce, onions, and pepper.

In a 2-quart casserole, layer one steak with sauce, then continue layering steaks and sauce until steaks are stacked one on top of the other. Add celery around the steaks.

Place temperature probe into the middle of the steaks. Cover with wax paper. Micro on 80 percent until the temperature reaches 140 degrees, about 15–20 minutes. About halfway through, rearrange the steaks so they cook evenly.

Cover with aluminum foil for 5 minutes before serving to continue cooking outside the oven.

Note: The meat will be a little pink when cooked in this manner. Cook to a higher temperature if you wish to have the meat well-done. My advice is to serve the meat a little pink inside so it doesn't toughen up.

ELK CHILIRONI

Serves 4–5

1 pound ground elk
1 small can tomato paste (6 ounces)
½ medium onion, chopped
2 cups water
1 tablespoon chili powder
¼ teaspoon red pepper
Salt, to taste
1 cup elbow macaroni (uncooked)
Grated cheese

In a 2-quart casserole, microwave ground elk for 6–7 minutes, stirring to break up the pieces every couple of minutes.

Add the rest of the ingredients to the elk. Stir well. Cover tightly and microwave on 50 percent or simmer for 15 minutes stirring two or three times.

Garnish with grated cheese.

Note: This is a quick and easy meal that my family has certainly enjoyed. If you wish, you could serve this over hamburger buns as sloppy joes or over hot dogs as chili dogs.

SAVORY ELK ROAST
Serves 5–6

1 3- or 4-pound elk roast
2 cloves garlic, slivered
¼ teaspoon rosemary
1 tablespoon olive oil
1 teaspoon ground sage
½ teaspoon ground black pepper
1 or 2 potatoes, cut in thick slices
½ cup dry red wine
½ cup beef broth or bouillon

Place the roast in a 2-quart casserole. Cut slits deep in the meat in various sections of the roast. Insert a sliver of garlic and a few pieces of rosemary.

Mix olive oil, sage, and pepper. Pour over the top and sides of the roast.

Arrange the potatoes around the roast. Mix the red wine and broth and pour over the potatoes.

Insert your microwave oven's temperature probe from the side into the inside of the roast. Cover loosely with plastic wrap. Cook at 50 percent or simmer until the inside of the roast reaches 130 degrees (about 20–30 minutes). Remove from the oven and cover with aluminum foil shiny side down to finish cooking. Allow to sit for 5 minutes before serving.

Note: You can thicken the drippings with a little flour if desired to thicken the gravy.

At 130 degrees, the roast will be cooked to medium rare on the inside. If you wish to have your roast cooked rare, cook it at 120 degrees or well-done to 140 degrees.

MARINATED ELK STEAK

Serves 2–4

1 large elk round steak, cut in either 2 or 4 serving pieces
½ pound whole mushrooms

Marinade:
½ cup Burgundy wine
1 teaspoon Worcestershire sauce
1 clove garlic, sliced
½ cup oil
2 tablespoons catsup
1 tablespoon vinegar
½ teaspoon marjoram
½ teaspoon Accent
½ teaspoon rosemary

Place elk pieces in the bottom of a glass baking dish. Place the mushrooms in the dish also.

In a small bowl, mix ingredients for marinade. Pour over the steak and mushrooms. Refrigerate overnight.

Remove the steak and mushrooms from the marinade and drain well. Place the steaks and the mushrooms in the glass baking dish. Cover loosely. Micro on 70 percent or roast for 10–12 minutes, turning the steaks over halfway through the cooking time.

Note: This is delicious. If you like the marinade, use it for broiled or barbecued steak also.

ELK STEAK PIZZAIOLA

Serves 2–4

1 large elk steak, cut into serving pieces
3 tablespoons olive oil
1 clove garlic, chopped
2 cups whole tomatoes, chopped
1 teaspoon oregano
½ teaspoon ground black pepper

In a heavy stovetop skillet, heat olive oil and add garlic. Cook garlic until just barely brown. Lightly brown the steaks for a minute or two in the hot oil. Remove the steaks from the oil and place in the bottom of an 8-inch glass baking dish.

Pour the tomatoes, oregano, and black pepper into the skillet. Bring to a boil and then simmer for 2–3 minutes. Pour the tomatoes and spices over the elk steaks in the baking dish. Cover loosely. Microwave on 70 percent for 5–7 minutes or until cooked to your tastes.

Allow to sit for a few minutes before serving.

Note: This is quick, tasty, and very visually appealing. Serve it with garlic bread and a green salad.

SWISS CHOPS

Serves 2

2 elk chops
4 tablespoons olive oil
1 large garlic clove, sliced
3 tablespoons Worcestershire sauce
4 tablespoons flour
2 carrots, sliced
2 celery stalks, sliced
1 cup beef bouillon
2 tablespoons steak sauce, such as A-1
3 tablespoons flour

In a heavy skillet heat the olive oil and the garlic. Cook the garlic until lightly browned, then stir in the Worcestershire sauce.

Dust the elk steaks lightly with flour. Add to the skillet. Brown lightly. Remove the elk steaks from the skillet and place in an 8-inch square baking dish. Add the carrots and celery. Stir well. Stir in the bouillon and the steak sauce. Bring to a boil and simmer for 2–3 minutes.

Remove ¼ cup of the hot liquid and stir the flour into it. Add the flour mixture to the carrots and celery, stirring until thickened.

Pour the sauce over the chops. Cover loosely. Micro on 70 percent or roast for 12–15 minutes until cooked to your desired liking. You should turn the chops over once or twice during the cooking time to allow them to cook evenly.

Note: This is a take-off on Swiss Steak, if you hadn't already figured it out. I find this recipe delicious. You could continue to cook the chops in the skillet, but I find they dry out and the vegetables often turn to mush if you do this. The microwave provides excellent results on this recipe quickly.

HAWAIIAN-STYLE ELK CHOPS
Serves 4

4 *elk chops*

Marinade:

1 13½-*ounce can pineapple chunks, packed in syrup, drained (reserve the syrup)*
¼ *cup soy sauce*
¼ *cup vinegar*
½ *teaspoon dry mustard*

1 *tablespoon oil*
¼ *cup brown sugar, packed*
1 *teaspoon cornstarch*

Place the chops in a glass baking dish. Stir together syrup from the pineapple, soy sauce, vinegar, and mustard. Pour over the chops. Marinade overnight.

Drain the chops, reserving the marinade. Heat oil in a heavy skillet and brown the chops. (Use your microwave browning dish if desired.)

Place the chops and ¼ cup of the marinade in a casserole dish. Cover loosely. Micro on 70 percent or roast for 15–18 minutes until the meat is cooked to your liking. Turn the chops over halfway through the cooking time. Remove chops from the oven and cover with foil, shiny side down, to finish cooking at least 5 minutes.

Mix sugar and cornstarch. Stir in remaining marinade. Micro on 50 percent for 4–5 minuutes until thickened. Add pineapple chunks.

Pour the sauce over the chops before serving.

Moose and Caribou

While moose are not taken as frequently as deer or elk in this country, there are plenty of hunters who seek this quarry every season.

There are moose seasons each year in states such as Alaska, Minnesota, Idaho, Utah, Wyoming, Maine, and in many parts of Canada. Hunters of moose in Maine were challenged by anti-hunters in a November 1983 ballot question that would have repealed the hunting season in Maine. The hunters won. Some of the hunts in the continental United States are very limited hunts, some are for residents only. A moose tag in some states is worth its weight in gold.

Bull moose are best when shot any other time of the year than when in the rut. The rutting period is normally from the middle of September to November. The meat of a bull moose in the rut is usually foul tasting.

Moose are the largest members of the deer family. Since their size is so large and the cuts of meat are undoubtedly larger than deer or antelope, the timing must be increased proportionally.

You'll know best, after cooking some of the meat, how to treat the rest of the animal. If you broil steaks and they turn out a little dry and tough, perhaps it would be best to brown them quickly in hot oil to seal in the juices. Then add a sauce to the dish and simmer the steaks in sauce.

A roast is better when you add some fat or cooking liquid to it. Pieces of salt pork can be inserted under the skin or broth added to the pot to steam the meat in liquid.

Caribou are probably even more rare in the game bag, but some lucky hunters do travel to Alaska and Canada to bring home this trophy animal and its fabulous meat. Caribou meat is juicy and tender due to the diet of the large animals. They feed on lichens and moss, horsetails and fungi, shrubs and saplings.

While the meat is overshadowed by the huge proportion of their massive antlers, if you have the opportunity to bag a caribou or to send your spouse after one, take full advantage of it. The trophy antlers and the delectable meat will be well worth the trip.

GERMAN-STYLE CARIBOU POT ROAST
Serves 6

4-pound caribou pot roast
2 tablespoons oil
½ teaspoon pepper
1 cup water
¼ cup flour
2 cloves garlic
Salt, to taste
Freshly ground black pepper, to taste
¼ teaspoon ginger
¼ cup catsup
2 tablespoons vinegar

In a large skillet, heat the oil and brown the outside of the caribou roast. Season with pepper. Remove to large casserole. Stir water into the skillet and scrape to remove the sediment. Pour water into casserole. Insert temperature probe into the center of the meat and micro on 70 percent or roast until the temperature reaches 130 degrees. Remove roast to platter and cover with foil shiny side down to finish cooking.

Blend flour with the juices in the casserole. Micro on 50 percent for 5 minutes. Stir in 2 cloves garlic, salt, pepper, ginger, catsup, and vinegar. Micro on 50 percent for 4–5 minutes. Pour gravy over the roast before serving.

MOOSE SAUERBRATEN
Serves 6

1 3–3½-pound moose chuck roast

Marinade:
1 onion, sliced
2 bay leaves
15 peppercorns
6 cloves
1 cup cider vinegar
½ cup boiling water

2 tablespoons oil
¾ cup gingersnaps, crushed
2 teaspoons sugar

Place roast in bowl with onion, bay leaves, peppercorns, cloves, vinegar, and boiling water. Cover tightly and refrigerate for at least 3 days. Turn the roast twice a day. Be careful not to pierce the meat when turning.

Drain the meat, reserving marinade. Heat oil in skillet and brown the roast on all sides. Remove meat to a clean, glass baking dish. Add marinade, insert the temperature probe and micro on 60 percent until temperature reaches 130–140 degrees (depending on how well you like the meat done). Remove meat and onions and cover with foil.

Strain the liquid in casserole and measure it. Add water if necessary to bring the total of liquid to 2 cups. Pour back into the casserole and micro on high for 3–4 minutes. Stir the gingersnaps and sugar into liquid. Micro on high for 2–3 minutes.

Serve meat and onions on a platter with the gingersnap gravy.

ROAST MOOSE WITH VEGETABLES
Serves 6–8

   3 tablespoons butter
   1 3- to 4-pound shoulder roast
  ¼ cup cognac
 10 small mushroom caps
 10 small white onions, peeled, but whole
   3 large carrots, cut into large pieces
   2 turnips, peeled and cut into chunks
   3 stalks celery, sliced
   1 tablespoon tomato paste
   3 tablespoons flour
   1 cup beef bouillon
  ¼ cup Burgundy wine
     Salt, to taste
     Freshly ground black pepper, to taste
   1 bay leaf

In a heavy skillet, heat 1 tablespoon butter and brown the roast. Heat the cognac, add to the meat and flame it. Remove meat from the pan.

In casserole, micro remaining butter. Add mushrooms, onions, carrots, turnips, and celery and micro on high for 5 minutes.

Add the tomato paste and flour. Stir well. Add the bouillon and wine. Micro on high for 5 minutes. Season with salt and pepper.

Place meat in casserole large enough to hold it. Add bay leaf and pour the vegetable mixture over the roast. Insert a temperature probe into the thickest part of meat. Be careful not to touch the bone with the probe. Cover loosely.

Micro on 60 percent until temperature reaches 130–140 degrees, depending on how well you like your meat cooked. Serve with vegetables.

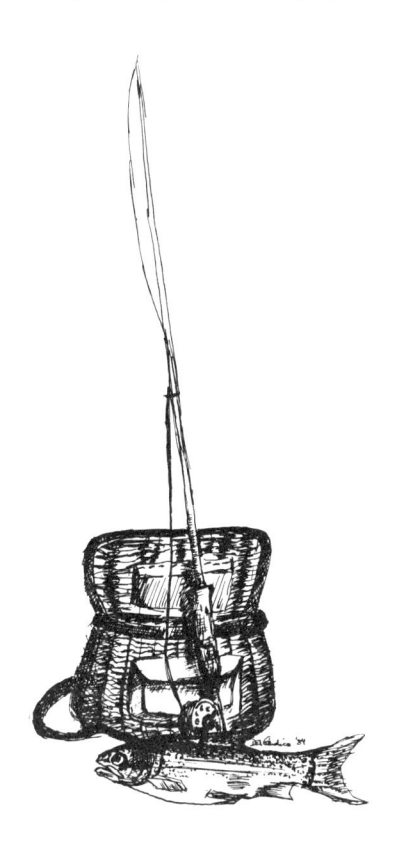

Fresh Water Catch

Bass

It's difficult to argue that bass are some of the jumpingest, fightingest, most explosive, rock 'em-sock 'em fish you can catch. Whether you enjoy fishing worms for largemouths or surface walking a Zara Spook over a school of thrashing stripers, most will agree the members of the bass family are exciting to fish.

When I was a young girl, my father's patients would bring us fillets of the largemouths they'd caught at the Ruby Marshes near Elko. Our family was a bunch of confirmed trout fishermen and I had no idea what a bass was. I'd never even seen a whole one since everyone brought fillets. I lived all those years near one of the best bass fisheries in Nevada and was ignorant of the excellent fishing there.

Then I moved to a town where there were even fewer bass fisheries. Trout were easy enough to find and again bass took a back seat.

The first largemouth I caught at Lake Mead was a dink. If it weighed a pound, I'd be surprised. But boy was I proud of that little fish. The second fish I tied into would give any bass fisherman a jolt of adrenaline. When he grabbed my Hot Shot and took to the sky, I knew he was definitely a good fish. When I got him near the boat, my fishing partner, Geoff Schneider with the Las Vegas News Bureau, was speechless. It was a good thing he was, too, or I probably would have never landed that bass.

The first thing that hog did was head for the weeds, but not before he gave us a good look at his heavy sides. I don't quite know how, but I managed to haul him out of the weeds. The gods of beginning bass fishermen were looking out for me, because I've never had to fight a fish diving for cover like that one.

When we finally netted that fish, Geoff told me, "If you were my wife, I'd give you a big kiss!" While that bass wasn't a state record or a line class record, at five pounds he looks dandy hanging on my wall watching down on me as I type this. It may take a while to catch another one that equals it in size or in importance. I *know* there are larger bass out there to catch and that first large one I ever landed has turned me into a confirmed bass fisherman.

It's also tough to decide whether I like fishing for largemouths or working topwater lures in a school of stripers inhaling shad. Well, it's a decision I'm reluctant to make. In any case, since one member of the bass family or another lives in every part of the United States and in some parts of Canada, there are many bass fishermen in our realm.

It's not difficult to decide that bass are some of the best eating of any fish anywhere. Bass are lean fish, there's not much oil in their meat, and they are usually very mild in taste. Someone who isn't crazy about eating trout because of their often strong flavor will probably enjoy the taste of bass.

Members of the bass family range in size from very small white bass to very large striped bass and there are numerous ways to handle cooking these fish. Most bass are filleted. Very small fillets can be steamed in the microwave or baked in your favorite recipes.

Recipes for rolled fish fillets work very well on bass. Recipes for baked whole fish, stuffed or not, will work on stripers in the five-pound range. If you catch a striper above the five-pound mark, which is common in many waters, you might cut the fillets in half and stuff them. A whole fish much above the five-pound range will not easily fit into your microwave and probably would be more suited to conventional methods of cooking.

Most fish can be interchanged in recipes. Perhaps you don't have any panfish handy for a recipe, but you do have some small white bass fillets or smallmouth fillets. Go ahead and use them. The flavor won't change much. Of course, you might have to adjust the cooking times, but that usually isn't critical. Just use the least amount of time necessary and adjust upwards if required.

Many bass fishermen now subscribe to the catch-and-release ideology. For those who don't want or need the fish for their tables, this is great as long as they follow the safest methods for releasing the fish. Some only release the excess fish, saving what they would like to have for dinner. I agree that fish of any kind should not be wasted and leave it up to you how to interpret that.

I like to eat bass, from largemouths to smallmouths to white bass to stripers, as much as I like to catch them. I especially like them fresh. So I'll take what I need for dinner and leave the rest behind. Besides, when I get a hankering for bass for dinner, it gives me a good excuse to go back and catch some more.

There are recipes here to tempt nearly everyone's taste buds. From Italian Bass Fillets to Bayou Bass, I'm sure you'll find something appealing.

ITALIAN BASS FILLETS
Serves 4

1½ pounds bass fillets
1 bell pepper, sliced
1 16-ounce can whole tomatoes, cut in chunks
¼ teaspoon summer savory
¼ teaspoon oregano
¼ teaspoon garlic powder
1¾ cup mozzarella cheese
Basil, fresh or dried

Combine peppers, tomatoes, savory, oregano, and garlic powder in small bowl.

In 1-quart casserole, spoon a little tomato mixture in the bottom of dish. Add 1 layer of fish fillets (cut to fit if necessary).

Spoon tomato mixture over fillets. Sprinkle cheese liberally over tomato mixture. Continue layering until ingredients are gone, ending up with tomato mixture and cheese on top. There should be 3 layers.

Microwave 13–15 minutes on bake or 50 percent power setting until middle of layer flakes. Cover with aluminum foil shiny side down for 4–5 minutes to finish cooking. Garnish with fresh or dried basil.

BAYOU BASS
Serves 4–5

    5 or 6 bass fillets, cut in bite-sized pieces (about 2 cups)
¼ teaspoon salt
¼ teaspoon turmeric
⅛ teaspoon cayenne
½ teaspoon paprika
½ teaspoon cumin
¼ teaspoon white pepper
3 tablespoons butter
1 cup onions, coarsely chopped
1 clove garlic, chopped
1 21-ounce can whole tomatoes, chopped (retain liquid)

Mix all spices in small bowl. In 2-quart casserole, microwave butter on high 1 minute. Add spices. Stir well. Micro on high 1½ minutes.

Stir in onions and garlic. Micro on high 2 minutes.

Add fish pieces. Stir in tomatoes and liquid. Cover tightly. Micro on high 5 minutes. Reduce power to 70 percent and micro for 5 minutes more. Let sit, covered, 5 minutes to finish cooking.

Serve in a bowl with lots of French bread to sop up the juice or serve on a bed of white rice.

Note: This dish is a little spicy. The amount of cayenne could be reduced to lower the "heat," if desired.

GLAZED BASS FILLETS
Serves 6

3 or 4 striped bass fillets
   Freshly ground black pepper
¼ cup lemon juice
3 tablespoons butter
2 tablespoons onion, grated
2 tablespoons brown sugar, firmly packed
1 teaspoon dry mustard
   Paprika
   Parsley flakes

Arrange fillets in a single layer in a shallow baking dish. Sprinkle with pepper.

In a small saucepan combine lemon juice, butter, onion, sugar, and dry mustard. Micro on high 1 minute. Pour over fish fillets.

Cover with plastic wrap. Micro on 70 percent or roast setting 8–10 minutes, until thickest part of the fish flakes easily.

Let stand, covered, 5 minutes before serving. Sprinkle with parsley flakes and paprika.

PESCE CON PESTO
Serves 4

1 cup cooked bass
2 cups fresh basil leaves
2 cloves garlic
¼ cup olive oil
3 tablespoons freshly grated Parmesan cheese
2 tablespoons pine nuts (or almonds)
1 pound cooked pasta

Process the basil and garlic in food processor or blender until leaves are finely chopped. Slowly pour in the olive oil.

Add cheese and nuts. Process until smooth in texture.

Toss the pesto with cooked pasta and cooked bass. The pesto sauce should thinly coat the pasta and fish, it shouldn't be dripping.

Note: I hope my Italian forefathers will forgive me for adding fish to this traditional cold pasta dish. I think the fish gives the dish a little extra lift, making this a delicious one-plate dish that is excellent for lunch or a light dinner. Finding something to do with leftover fish is often a chore. This is a tasty way to use leftovers. Even leftover pasta, warmed a few minutes in the microwave, works well.

CREAMY BASS
Serves 4–6

1½ pounds bass fillets
½ cup light cream
Salt, to taste
Freshly ground black pepper
¼ teaspoon nutmeg
Minced parsley
Paprika
Tartar sauce

Arrange bass fillets in a single layer in the bottom of a glass baking dish.

Combine the remaining ingredients except parsley and tartar sauce. Pour over the fillets. Cover tightly. Micro on 70 percent or roast for 8–10 minutes, until fish barely flakes. Remove from oven and cover with foil, shiny side down, to finish cooking.

Garnish with minced parsley and paprika. Serve with tartar sauce.

STRIPED BASS ROLLS
Serves 2–4

4 striped bass fillets
4 tablespoons breadcrumbs
4 tablespoons grated Parmesan cheese
1 tablespoon chopped capers
½ tomato, cut in chunks
Salt and pepper, to taste
3–4 tablespoons melted butter
2 cups tomato sauce

Mix together breadcrumbs, cheese, capers, tomato, salt and pepper, and enough melted butter to obtain a paste.

Spread evenly over fillets. Roll them and secure with toothpicks or string.

Place rolls in 2-quart casserole and pour the tomato sauce over fish. Cover loosely. Micro on 70 percent or roast for 5–7 minutes, turning the dish once during cooking time. Remove from microwave and cover with aluminum foil, shiny side down, for 2–3 minutes before serving.

Catfish

Catfish are about as maligned as antelope are. In some parts of the country they are the only game fish within a reasonable driving distance to go after. In other states they are lowered to the status of trash fish in the eyes of some of the unknowing anglers. In some areas they are treated with the respect they deserve.

One thing is for certain, nearly everywhere you go you're bound to find some catfish to fish for. They're accessible to nearly everyone. Another certain thing is in many areas of the country, you won't be fishing elbow-to-elbow with other people because some fishermen are ignorant of the fun of catfishing and the glories of fresh catfish fillets.

We all know the traditional way of cooking catfish is to dredge catfish fillets in a breading, usually cornmeal but sometimes flour, then pop them in hot oil until they're golden brown and crispy. Boy, my mouth waters thinking about it.

Try as I did I couldn't even come close to that kind of a catfish recipe in the microwave. So as not to be called sacrilegious, I didn't include any recipes for what might be called shake and bake. If you can't do it right, and that means frying catfish, don't try to fake it.

There are a few other things you can do with those whole catfish or fillets, though, and I've given you a few alternatives here.

I suspect the reason why catfishing is unpopular in areas is because I'll bet half the anglers who catch a catfish don't know what to do with one once they've caught it. In fact, I'm very certain that's the case because I've been one of those fishermen who caught a catfish by accident and didn't have the foggiest notion what to do with it then, so I gave it away.

After that, I did a lot of researching into the ways of the wily whiskered fish and learned what to do with one if I were to catch one again. I was prepared to handle 'em and skin 'em and cook 'em the next time I fished for my bewhiskered friend.

If I can't get out to fish for them, I know I can go down to the local fish market and pick up some there. I guess the local people around here like to eat fried catfish and hush puppies more than they like to catch catfish, which is fine with me. I'd much rather stand in line in a fish market than in line at my catfishing hole.

My father claims he likes the catfish recipes better than those for most other fish he's tried in conjunction with the birth of this cookbook.

Although I've found the catfish I've eaten that were freshly caught have a slightly different flavor, maybe a little muddier, than those prepared for commercial distribution, this really doesn't make a whole lot of difference in the taste or quality of the fish. I've heard that soaking the fish in water for several hours before cooking it can remove the muddy flavor. I'd try some salt in the water as well. But be careful to rinse the salt water off the fish thoroughly before cooking.

GARLIC CATFISH
Serves 2

2 catfish, 1½–2 pounds each
⅓ cup olive oil
1 tablespoon garlic, minced
¼ cup white wine
¼ cup dry sherry
Juice from ½ lemon
1 teaspoon basil
1 teaspoon oregano
¼ teaspoon dry red pepper, crushed
2 cups tomatoes, chopped

In microproof bowl or saucepan, pour in olive oil and add garlic. Micro on high for 2 minutes. Pour in wine and sherry. Add the lemon juice and stir in the basil, oregano, and red pepper. Add tomatoes and micro on 50 percent for 10 minutes.

Place the catfish in baking dish. Pour the sauce over the catfish and cover loosely. Micro on 70 percent or roast for 15–18 minutes until fish barely flakes. Remove from oven and cover with foil, shiny side down, for 5 minutes before serving.

CATFISH WITH MUSHROOMS AND BUTTERMILK
Serves 4

4 catfish, about 1½ pounds each
4 tablespoons butter
1 tablespoon onion, chopped
2 cups mushrooms
2½ cups buttermilk
  Salt, to taste
  Freshly ground black pepper, to taste
4 ounces cream cheese
2 teaspoons parsley flakes

In microproof saucepan, micro butter 1 minute on high. Stir in onions and mushrooms. Micro on high 5-6 minutes or until mushrooms are thoroughly cooked. Stir in 1½ cups of the buttermilk, salt, and pepper.

Arrange catfish in a casserole large enough to hold them. Pour onions and mushrooms over the top of the fish. Cover loosely. Micro on 70 percent or roast for 18-20 minutes until fish just barely flakes.

Remove fish (drain off the juices but retain the mushrooms and the onions, set aside) and place on platter. Cover with foil, shiny side down, for at least 5 minutes before serving.

Meanwhile, mix mushrooms and onions with 4 ounces cream cheese and 1 cup buttermilk. Micro on 50 percent for 3 minutes or until the cream cheese is combined with buttermilk and the sauce is warm. Add parsley flakes and stir well. Spoon over catfish.

CATFISH IN HORSERADISH SAUCE
Serves 2

2 catfish, 1½–2 pounds each
2 egg whites
2 tablespoons sour cream
2 tablespoons onions, chopped
1 clove garlic, minced
¼ teaspoon basil
½ teaspoon freshly ground black pepper
2 tablespoons butter
2 tablespoons flour
1 cup milk
2 tablespoons horseradish
1 teaspoon paprika

Arrange fish in a casserole. In a small bowl, beat egg whites until soft peaks form. Fold in sour cream, onion, garlic, basil, and ¼ teaspoon pepper. Spoon over the catfish.

Cover tightly and micro on 70 percent or roast for 15–17 minutes until fish barely flakes. Remove from oven and cover with aluminum foil, shiny side down, while making sauce.

In small bowl, micro butter 1 minute on high. Add flour, stirring until smooth. Gradually stir in milk with whisk. Add horseradish, paprika, and ¼ teaspoon pepper. Micro on 80 percent or reheat for 3–4 minutes until sauce is thickened, stirring once or twice.

Spoon sauce over fish. Serve with additional horseradish for those who like it hot.

Note: This is a very good way of preparing catfish.

CATFISH FILLETS
Serves 2–4

4 medium catfish fillets
¼ cup cracker crumbs
¼ cup plus 2 tablespoons Parmesan cheese
Salt, to taste
Freshly ground black pepper, to taste
1 10-ounce package frozen spinach
¾ cup buttermilk salad dressing
2 tablespoons lemon juice
1 8-ounce package cream cheese
¼ cup buttermilk salad dressing
½ teaspoon dry mustard
½ teaspoon tarragon

Flatten the fillets. Mix crumbs, 2 tablespoons Parmesan cheese, salt, and pepper in a flat dish. Coat fillets with crumb mixture.

Cut frozen spinach into quarters. Place one quarter of the spinach in each fillet and roll up the fillets.

In a 9-inch square baking dish, pour ½ cup of the buttermilk dressing. Place the rolled fillets on top of buttermilk mixture.

In medium bowl, mix lemon juice, cream cheese, ¼ cup dressing, dry mustard, tarragon, and ¼ cup Parmesan cheese. Spoon over the top of the fillets.

Cover loosely. Micro on 70 percent or roast for 12–15 minutes, until fish barely flakes.

Serve with lemon wedges.

Panfish

If squirrels and rabbits are the traditional quarry of young, beginning hunters, then panfish such as crappie and bluegills are comparable as the beginning catch for young anglers. It is said that the memories of those beginning experiences with the outdoors lure us back after we've become adults. Perhaps that's why so many adults enjoy the simple pleasures of catching these diminutive treasures.

Bluegills, members of the sunfish family, are so adept at reproducing that often ponds where they live become overpopulated, causing stunting of their bodies. This is an ideal situation for the angler because of the sheer numbers of the population. But if you're looking for a larger fish, you'll want to head for waters where there aren't as many fish.

Other members of the sunfish family are redear sunfish, pumpkinseeds, redbreast sunfish, warmouth, green sunfish, and longear sunfish. They are all widespread and there are probably at least two or three varieties in your area.

Crappies also belong to the sunfish family. They range over the entire country, except for a few states in the Rocky Mountain area. Crappies can be easily caught. But then again, they might be as fickle as any fish species known. They're more wary than bluegills so they're often more difficult to catch, especially in clear water.

While worms are probably the most widespread bait on bluegills, minnows are the sure bet on crappies. Jigs work well also. Spinners tipped with bait are often used.

Fishing for panfish should not be underestimated. There are many good reasons for foresaking large, whopper-sized fish for small panfish. Taking a child fishing is one good reason to explore your memories of a time long ago, perhaps when you learned to fish.

I wasn't fortunate enough to have a bluegill pond to practice on when I was growing up. I practiced on loosing rooster tails in trout streams around my home town. It took me the longest time to honestly catch a fish (that means baiting the hook, hooking the fish, and reeling him in all alone). I guess even the unfortunate go straight in the long run. I love fishing for panfish now.

Another good reason is to try new tricks on these old friends. Who knows? Maybe you'll come up with a method for panfishing no one's ever used before.

One of the best reasons I can think of is because panfish taste so good. Although you'll probably have to catch a bunch to satisfy the hearty appetites worked up after a day of hard bluegill or crappie fishing, the effort is well worth it. Your children will love eating them as much as they love catching them. Oh, you'll love them, too. Maybe they'll bring back the kid in you!

GINGERED PANFISH FILLETS

Serves 2–3

1–1½ pounds bluegill fillets
1 tablespoon butter
1 clove garlic, chopped
1 teaspoon ground ginger
1½ tablespoons sugar
2½ tablespoons soy sauce
1 tablespoon cornstarch
6 tablespoons water
2 green onions, cut thinly

Arrange fillets in glass baking dish, cover with plastic wrap. Steam them in microwave on 70 percent 5 minutes. Remove from oven and allow to sit 5 minutes. Then transfer to warm plate.

Micro butter in small saucepan on high for 1 minute. Stir in garlic, ginger, sugar, and soy sauce. In separate bowl, mix cornstarch and water. Add cornstarch to ginger mixture. Stir well.

Micro on 50 percent for 2 minutes, or until thickened, stirring occasionally. Pour sauce over fillets. Sprinkle green onion on top as a garnish.

Note: This is delicious and very spicy. If you don't like so much ginger, reduce the amount by half.

PANFISH PARMIGIANA
Serves 4–6

1 pound panfish fillets
   Salt and freshly ground black pepper, to taste
1 cup tomato sauce
½ cup Parmesan cheese
1 tablespoon butter, melted
   Parsley sprigs

Place fish in a single layer in baking dish large enough to hold them. Season with salt and pepper, if desired.

Spread tomato sauce over the fillets.

Sprinkle Parmesan cheese over the fillets. Drizzle butter evenly over the cheese.

Cover loosely. Micro on 80 percent or reheat for 5–8 minutes until fish barely flakes. Remove from oven and cover with foil, shiny side down, for 5 minutes before serving. Garnish with parsley sprigs.

FISH ROLLS

Serves 4

2 pounds bluegill or crappie fillets
¼ cup butter
2 tablespoons onion, finely chopped
2 cups soft bread crumbs
½ cup walnuts, chopped
2 stalks celery, finely chopped
2 tablespoons parsley, finely chopped
  Salt, to taste
  Freshly ground black pepper, to taste
3 tablespoons water
3 tablespoons butter, melted
  Lemon wedges

In a medium saucepan, micro butter on high for 1 minute. Stir in onion and micro on high 2 minutes. Stir in bread crumbs, walnuts, celery, parsley, salt, and pepper. Sprinkle with water and stir well.

Spread mixture on each fillet and roll them up. Place seam sides down in a 9-inch square casserole. Drizzle butter over the top of the fillets.

Cover loosely. Micro on 70 percent or roast for 12–15 minutes until fish just barely flakes. Remove from oven and cover with foil, shiny side down, for 3-5 minutes.

Serve with lemon wedges.

PANFISH CASSEROLE

Serves 4

2 pounds panfish fillets
1 onion, chopped
2 cups whole tomatoes, chopped
½ bell pepper, chopped
  Salt, to taste
  Freshly ground black pepper, to taste
¼ teaspoon basil
  Rice

Place the fillets in the bottom of a glass baking dish large enough to hold them.

Combine onion, tomatoes, bell pepper, salt, pepper, and basil. Stir well. Pour over the fillets. Cover tightly. Micro on 80 percent or reheat for 6–9 minutes, until fish barely flakes. Remove from oven and cover with foil, shiny side down, for 3–5 minutes before serving.

Serve over rice.

PANFISH ALBERTI
Serves 4

2 pounds panfish fillets
1 cup dry vermouth
3 tablespoons green onion, chopped
2 tablespoons fresh parsley, chopped
   Salt, to taste
   Freshly ground black pepper, to taste
1 cup butter, cut into small pieces
8 egg yolks
2 tablespoons heavy cream

In a baking dish, micro the vermouth, green onions, and parsley on high for 3 minutes. Add the fillets, dust with salt and pepper, cover, and poach on 70 percent or roast for 5–8 minutes until the fish barely flakes.

Remove the fish to a plate and cover with foil.

Pour out half the cooking liquid. Mix the remaining half of the cooking liquid with the butter and egg yolks. Micro the sauce on 40 percent until sauce thickens, whisking it every minute or so. Add the cream. Pour over the fillets.

If desired, broil for a few minutes to glaze.

BROCHETTES OF BLUEGILL

Serves 4

1-1½ pounds bluegill fillets, cut into chunks
2 zucchini, sliced thickly
16 mushroom caps

Marinade:

2 teaspoons olive oil
1 clove garlic, minced
1 bay leaf, crumbled
2 teaspoons lemon juice

8 wooden skewers
Lemon wedges

Mix fish pieces, zucchini, and mushrooms together.

Combine marinade ingredients and pour over the fish mixture. Marinade for 1 hour.

Thread the fish and vegetables, alternating them, on the skewers. Place the skewers on a bacon rack or place them over the center of a bowl with the edges of the skewers balancing on the lip of the bowl.

Cover loosely and micro on 70 percent or roast for 8 minutes.

Serve with lemon wedges.

Salmon

Even though salmon can be found in only a few parts of the United States, it is one of the most favorite fish both to eat and to catch. Many people have experience with eating salmon even if they aren't fortunate enough to fish for salmon, because it is widely available in several forms.

Fish markets and even the seafood departments of grocery stores carry seasonal supplies of salmon. You can buy whole salmon, steaked salmon, or filleted salmon. If you can't find any fresh salmon, you can buy canned, smoked, or kippered salmon. Most restaurants serve salmon year-round. No matter where we live, we can buy salmon.

Of course, this helps the popularity of the fish and makes it widely available to all of us commercially. But in my own mind, I'm convinced you haven't tasted salmon until you catch your own fresh-from-the-sea salmon. Fresh salmon is just out of this world.

I had always dreamt about fishing Alaska. Several years ago at a fishing show in San Francisco, I watched a promotional movie on fishing Alaska and couldn't believe what I was seeing. Tears ran down my face. I'd never seen anything more incredibly beautiful, so remote, so primitive, so exciting as I found in those films. I was struck with an immense case of wanderlust.

Within six months of that date, I was aboard Wien airlines on my way to King Salmon, Alaska, with my final destination the Alagnak River. It was during the month of August and I'd timed my arrival absolutely without a flaw. I figured I'd be just missing the king salmon run, but I was lucky enough to catch the tail end of it while there were still some fresh (chrome) kings coming in the river.

Not only that but the silver salmon run was beginning. I was in heaven. If that wasn't enough, we ate very well thanks to Jim and Julie Maxwell. I was there for a week and I figure I ate salmon for eighty percent of my meals and you wouldn't hear one squeak of a complaint out of me.

We had salmon omelettes in the morning, salmon sandwiches at lunch, and salmon pie for dinner. It was a salmon lover's paradise or enough to turn anyone into a devout salmon lover.

As it is with so many different types of fish, it is hard for me to decide which I like better—catching or eating them. With salmon it's equally difficult. While I was in Alaska, I caught coho or silver salmon, chum or dog salmon, and chinook or king salmon. I can tell that I like catching kings more than any other variety of the group.

I lucked into a pretty decent salmon while in Alaska. A little, old 43-pounder took my lure and tried to bury it in the sand in the delta. When I hooked into him, I really had some difficulty holding it together.

I set the hook hard, twice, according to my guide's instructions. Then the adrenaline hit me. I stood up too quickly to set the hook and nearly passed out, then a huge adrenaline rush hit and I nearly lost my lunch right there. I was desperately afraid I was going to lose this big fish and all my bragging rights along with him. I said my prayers and kept on reeling. The third time he came to the boat we netted him—a fish almost too big for me to hold up for the pictures.

That provided some mighty good eating for my family during the cold winter months back in Reno when wanderlust turned my mind back on Alaska. In fact, many of these recipes were tested on the meat I carried back with me from the Last Frontier.

There are many ways to cook salmon in the microwave, but probably the one most suited to it is poaching. Poached salmon is absolutely delightful and very simple to do. Serve poached salmon with any of a number of sauces such as hollandaise or hot mustard or tartar sauce.

You can marinade and then steam the steaks. Once you've cooked the salmon, there are numerous recipes for cooked salmon. In fact, even if you decide to use conventional recipes for cooking salmon, if you find one that calls for cooked salmon and what you've got just came out of the water, then steam it for a few minutes in the microwave before adding it to your recipe.

You can dress salmon up or dress it down, but even the simplest of salmon recipes will be exceptional.

If you buy salmon in a market, make certain it is the freshest you can get. Ask the grocer if you can smell the fish. This is the easiest way to make sure. But if you can, spend some time fishing for salmon. They are incredible fish to hook into and they fight like the dickens. Any size is a trophy in my book, but if you're looking for really big salmon you ought to go to Alaska.

SALMON QUICHE
Serves 4

1 cup flaked, poached salmon (canned salmon could be used)
1 9-inch pie crust
3 tablespoons oil
2 cloves garlic, sliced
2 stalks broccoli, chopped (about 2 cups)
4 eggs
¼ cup milk
¼ cup chopped onion
2 cups grated mozzarella cheese
⅓ cup chopped chives

Combine oil and garlic in small microproof saucepan, add broccoli. Cover lightly. Micro on high 2 minutes. Stir. Micro 2 minutes more on high setting.

Beat eggs slightly in mixing bowl. Add ¼ cup milk. Stir in onion, salmon, cheese, and broccoli. Pour into pie shell.

Micro on roast or medium setting for 11–13 minutes or just until the middle is set. Don't overcook.

Remove from oven and cover with foil, shiny side down. Let sit for 5 minutes or so to finish cooking. Garnish the edges near the pie crust crimp with chopped chives.

Note: Eggs get as tough as corrugated cardboard if overcooked.

FETTUCINE AL SALMON
Serves 6

1 cup packed, flaked, cooked salmon drained
   (should be about 2 cups salmon before packing)
6 tablespoons butter
1 clove garlic, chopped finely
6 tablespoons flour
2 cups Half & Half
1 pound fettucine noodles, cooked and drained
   Fresh parsley

Put butter in medium microproof saucepan. Micro on high setting about 1 minute or until melted. Stir in garlic and salmon. Add flour and stir thoroughly. Add 2 cups Half & Half.

Micro on high 4–6 minutes uncovered until desired thickness. Stir thoroughly every minute until cooking is complete.

Spoon over drained noodles. Garnish with fresh parsley.

POACHED SALMON STEAKS
Serves 4

4 small salmon steaks or 2 large steaks
1½ cups hot water
1 cup dry white wine
4 peppercorns
2 slices onion
   Salt, to taste

Mix hot water, wine, peppercorns, onion slices, and salt in casserole large enough to hold the salmon steaks in single layer. Microwave on high 5 minutes.

Place steaks in hot liquid. Cover. Microwave on high 3–4 minutes or until fish becomes opaque.

Serve with clarified butter, low-cal dill sauce, or mustard hollandaise. (See my recipes in the section on Sauces, Butters, and Marinades.)

GARLIC SALMON
Serves 4

2 large salmon steaks or 4 small steaks
3 tablespoons butter
3 tablespoons olive oil
2 tablespoons lemon juice
2 tablespoons garlic, minced
1 teaspoon fresh tarragon or ½ teaspoon dried tarragon
¼ teaspoon freshly grated lemon peel
⅛ teaspoon cayenne pepper
1 tablespoon sesame seeds
Lemon and lime wedges

In small microproof bowl, melt butter by microwaving on high for 1 minute. Combine remaining ingredients except sesame seeds, salmon steaks, and lemon and lime wedges.

Arrange salmon steaks in baking dish large enough to hold them in a single layer. Pour lemon mixture over top of steaks. Cover with plastic wrap. Make tight seal with wrap. Micro on high for 5–7 minutes until fish becomes opaque.

Remove from oven and cover with aluminum foil shiny side down to finish cooking. Sprinkle with sesame seeds and garnish with lemon and lime wedges before serving.

QUICK SALMON CASSEROLE
Serves 4

16 ounces cooked salmon
1½ cups elbow macaroni
1 16-ounce can cream style corn
¾ cup onion, chopped
1 8-ounce can peas, drained
1 cup shredded cheddar cheese

Cook macaroni as directed on package and drain well. Add corn, onion, and peas to macaroni. Mix well.

Cover and microwave on high 5 minutes. Add salmon and microwave on high 3 minutes more. Stir in cheese. Microwave on high 1 minute to melt cheese.

Note: This is a great last-minute dinner dish or a hearty lunch.

STUFFED SALMON STEAKS
Serves 2-4

2 large salmon steaks
3 tablespoons butter
1 slice onion, chopped
1 tablespoon fresh parsley, chopped
1 slice bread, crumbled
1 cup mushrooms, finely sliced
  Salt and freshly ground black pepper, to taste
½ cup light cream
  Parsley, chopped

Micro 2½ tablespoons butter in small bowl on high for 1 minute. Add onions and parsley and micro on high 3-4 minutes.

In the bowl with the onions, mix bread, mushrooms, salt, and pepper.

In a glass baking dish arrange one salmon steak in the bottom. Spread the mixture over the steak. Cover with the second steak. Pour the cream over the top. Dot with remaining butter. Cover loosely.

Micro on 70 percent or roast for 10-15 minutes until the bottom steak just barely flakes.

Remove from oven and cover with aluminum foil for 4-5 minutes to allow fish to finish cooking.

Garnish with chopped parsley.

BAKED SALMON
Serves 2

    2 *large salmon steaks*
      Salt and freshly ground black pepper, to taste
    2 *tablespoons butter, melted*
    1 *tablespoon parsley, chopped*
      Lemon slices

Sprinkle both sides of steaks with salt and pepper. Place steaks in baking dish large enough to hold them. Brush with butter.

Combine remaining butter with parsley. Set aside.

Cover steaks loosely. Micro on roast or 70 percent for 8–10 minutes, until steaks barely flake in the center. (It may take more time, depending on thickness of steaks.)

Remove from microwave and cover with foil, shiny side down to finish cooking, for 3–5 minutes.

Serve the steaks with parsley butter and lemon slices.

FLORENTINE SALMON
Serves 4

    2 *cups salmon, cooked*
¼–½ *cup milk*
    ¼ *cup butter*
    ¼ *cup flour*
    ½ *teaspoon dry mustard*
    ½ *teaspoon Tabasco*
 1½ *cups grated mozzarella cheese*
    1 *10-ounce package frozen spinach, thawed and drained*

Drain salmon, retaining the liquid and adding to it enough milk to make 1 cup. Flake the drained salmon.

In a medium saucepan, micro butter 1 minute on high. Add flour and stir with a whisk. Set aside.

Pour salmon liquid into small saucepan and microwave on high for 2 minutes. Pour all at once into flour and butter mixture, stirring with whisk until thickened. (If the mixture is not the consistency of mayonnaise, micro on 70 percent or roast for 2–3 minutes until thickened. Stir once or twice.) Add mustard, Tabasco, and 1 cup of the grated cheese.

Place the spinach in the bottom of a medium casserole dish and place the salmon in a layer over the spinach. Spread the cream sauce over the salmon and sprinkle with the remaining grated cheese.

Cover tightly and microwave on 70 percent for 8–10 minutes or until heated through.

Note: The taste of this is very subtle. I enjoy eating this dish as much as I enjoy fishing for salmon. If you plan to serve this for company, you might use individual casserole dishes, if you have some that will work in the microwave.

Trout

Members of the trout family provide some of the best fishing found in North America. Even the most fanatical catch and release fisherman will usually save a trout or two to cook for a meal.

While, admittedly, most of the trout caught never make it home to the kitchen, the ones that do are easily suited to microwave cooking.

The fish that don't make it home to your kitchen usually succumb to the hot coals of a camper's cook fire as a shore lunch, and there are few who would argue that freshly caught trout make a fine breakfast when fired quickly over glowing embers. Trout are also a good choice for smoking, canning, or pickling. But after you've tried a few of the recipes in this cookbook, you'll have to agree the microwave does one fine job on these fish.

Because trout range over such a large part of North America, they are probably the most popular catch of any freshwater fish. Nearly every angler has trout stashed away in the freezer ready to cook. Even though they are so much fun to catch, an angler who doesn't have access to any fresh trout can buy them in most good fish markets.

Usually the best meals are made of pan-sized trout, although there are plenty of trout fishermen who would agree with me that large fish are excellent when stuffed and baked or poached. I've caught five-pound or better cutthroats that are excellent when microwaved.

Trout, whether they're small or large, are oily fish and deserve a little special treatment. A great amount of cooking liquid is not necessary when microwaving trout since they come packed with their own oil in their tissues. If they're overcooked, though, as is common with microwave cooking, they will turn into dry, tasteless morsels—a real shame to lose a fish as beautiful as a trout unnecessarily.

When you cook large fish such as lake trout, it's best to trim away some of the fatty deposits often found on the bellies of the fish if possible. Since little extra fluid is needed, the fat is not necessary and may ruin the delicate taste of the trout.

Depending on where the fish are caught, the meat of the cooked trout will range from a creamy white to salmon-colored pink. This comes from the fish's eating habits. Those with pink meat feed on freshwater shrimp. In my opinion, the meat on the fish feeding on these shrimp is excellent—hard to beat.

The size of your microwave can be the limiting factor when you cook the larger species of trout. In this case, I'd cut the fish in pieces to fit the cookware you use in your microwave.

Trout are easily poached or steamed in the microwave in a short period of time and can be served with any number of sauces found later in this book. Some people aren't crazy about the taste of the fish and in that case I'd serve a sauce with a stronger flavor. For those who like to eat trout, a mild sauce won't hide the taste of the fish.

Although a large amount of aluminum foil is not recommended for the microwave due to conduction problems, a small amount of foil won't hurt your oven. You may choose, therefore, to cover the heads and tails of the fish so they won't overcook. I haven't done this with any of the recipes I've served and they turn out just as appetizing as the fish that have been shielded.

It's also wise to cover the fish well to avoid the popping that happens when an oily fish is cooked at a high setting in the microwave. Lowering the power setting reduces the popping to some extent, but it's easier to cover the fish than it is to pry cooked matter from the inside of the oven.

Choosing my favorite species of trout is a tough one. I've caught large cutthroats at the world famous Pyramid Lake and hauled lake trout from 200 feet off the bench bottoms of Lake Tahoe. From a high Sierra trout stream with its magnificent rainbow fishing to the awesome huge rainbows in an Alaskan trophy trout stream, I've been fortunate to sample the wares. My favorite eating fish? Well, hands down it comes to the small brook trout the size of my outstretched hand with its delicate meat tucked beneath a tiny framework of bones.

Whatever your favorite species of trout may be, you'll most certainly agree the microwave oven and the trout are worthy comrades.

TARRAGON TROUT
Serves 2

    2 trout, pan dressed, each 1–1½ pounds, cut off heads and tails so they'll fit into dish, if desired
    2 tablespoons butter
    Salt and pepper, to taste
¼ cup dry white wine
    2 carrots, sliced
    2 stalks celery, sliced
¼ teaspoon tarragon
¼ teaspoon basil
½ teaspoon fresh parsley, chopped
    Lemon slices

Micro butter in large glass baking dish 1 minute on high. Add fish with belly sides facing each other. Salt and pepper insides and outsides of fish, if desired. Pour wine over fish. Add sliced carrots and celery.

Sprinkle tarragon, basil, and parsley over fish and vegetables. Cover well. Micro 4 minutes on high. Turn dish. Micro 4 minutes more on high.

Remove from microwave and cover with foil, shiny side toward fish, for several minutes to finish cooking.

Garnish with fresh lemon slices.

MUSHROOM STUFFED TROUT
Serves 2

2 trout, pan dressed, 1–1½ pounds each
½ teaspoon salt
¼ teaspoon white pepper
2 tablespoons melted butter

Stuffing:
1 cup mushrooms, chopped
½ medium onion, chopped
2 stalks celery, chopped
½ cup butter, melted
¼ cup fresh parsley, chopped
1 teaspoon thyme, crushed
2 slices fresh bread, crumbled
Lemon slices

Sprinkle salt and pepper on inside and outside of fish. Brush with butter and place in microproof dish just large enough to hold fish.

Sauté mushrooms, onion, and celery in butter 2 minutes on high setting in microwave. Combine remaining ingredients (except lemon slices). Mix well and use to stuff fish.

Cover the stuffed fish. Bake on high setting in microwave 8 minutes, turning once during cooking time. Remove from microwave and cover immediately with foil, shiny side down, to complete cooking for 2–4 minutes.

Serve with fresh lemon slices.

CRAB STUFFED TROUT
Serves 2

2 trout, 1–1½ pounds each
1 clove garlic, minced
1 bunch green onions, sliced
1 stalk celery, thinly sliced
2 tablespoons butter
1 12-ounce can crabmeat, drained and flaked
½ cup fresh parsley, minced
1 piece of fresh bread, crumbled
1 egg, lightly beaten
1 teaspoon Dijon mustard
  Juice of ½ lemon
  Salt and pepper, to taste

Combine garlic, green onions, celery, and butter in microwave saucepan. Cover and micro on high 2 minutes. Add crabmeat, parsley, bread, egg, mustard, lemon juice, salt and pepper to taste. Mix well.

Place fish in a shallow microwave casserole just large enough to hold them with the head of one facing the tail of the other and the bellies facing toward the center.

Divide the stuffing between the fish and close opening as much as possible. Cover tightly with plastic wrap and micro 8 minutes on high, turning fish over and rearranging halfway through the cooking time.

Remove from microwave. Cover with aluminum, shiny side down, and let sit 2–3 minutes to finish cooking.

HERBED TROUT AND MACARONI SALAD
Serves 8–10

1 cup flaked trout
4 cups egg twistees macaroni, cooked (12-ounce package)

Dressing:
½ cup oil
½ cup vinegar
1 egg
4 tablespoons mayonnaise
¼ teaspoon oregano
¼ teaspoon tarragon
¼ teaspoon basil
¼ teaspoon dill weed

1 cup green beans
1 carrot, sliced
1 cup corn
1 cup cauliflower florets
2–3 tablespoons water

Cook noodles al dente (until firm), drain thoroughly, and chill well.

Make dressing well ahead of serving time, too. Mix oil, vinegar, egg, mayonnaise, oregano, tarragon, basil, and dill weed. Stir well. Chill.

Mix green beans, carrot, corn, and cauliflower in medium bowl. Add 2–3 tablespoons water. Cover well. Micro on high 4 minutes. Stir once while cooking. Chill thoroughly.

When all ingredients are cool, combine fish, noodles, and vegetables. Toss well. Chill until ready to serve. Pour dressing over salad. Toss and serve.

WILDHORSE RATATOUILLE TROUT
Serves 4

4 trout, pan dressed
4 tablespoons oil
1 clove garlic, minced
1 large onion, coarsely chopped
2 green peppers, sliced into strips
2 large tomatoes, chopped
4 small or 2 medium zucchini, chopped into chunks
1 small eggplant, peeled and chopped into chunks
1 tablespoon tomato paste
Freshly ground pepper, to taste

In 2-quart casserole or glass bowl, mix oil, garlic, and onions. Stir well. Cover. Micro on high 5 minutes.

Add peppers, tomatoes, zucchini, eggplant, tomato paste, and ground pepper to taste. Stir well to combine. Cover. Micro on high 10 minutes.

Arrange trout in a glass baking dish large enough to hold them in a single layer. Pour vegetable mixture over trout. Cover. Micro on 70 percent or roast setting 10–12 minutes, until thickest part of the fish flakes easily. Let sit, covered, 5 minutes before serving.

Note: You'll be surprised at how moist the fish is cooked in this recipe.

SCUFFY'S CAMP BROOKIES

Serves 3–4

12 brook trout, pan dressed
4 tablespoons butter
1 red bell pepper, grated
½ medium onion, grated
Freshly ground pepper, to taste

Arrange fish in single layer in baking dish just large enough to hold them comfortably. The thickest parts of the fish should face toward the outside of the dish on all sides to assure even cooking.

In a small saucepan or bowl, microwave butter 1 minute on high to melt. Add red bell pepper, onion, and ground pepper. Stir well to combine.

Spread mixture evenly over trout. Cover with plastic wrap.

Microwave on high 7–8 minutes or until fish flakes easily. Allow to sit a few minutes before serving to finish cooking.

Note: High in the Nevada mountains is a brook trout stream where the water is clear, the people are few, and the trout unpressured. In this coveted spot the brookies are easily fooled by a fly or a worm and hook, tied to a horse tail hair line, attached to a well-chosen willow branch.

Those who've shared a meal of these trout cooked up at Scuffy's claim these to be the sweetest, tastiest trout in the Silver State. This cookbook wouldn't be complete without dedicating a recipe to those fishermen responsible for introducing me to Scuffy's and these trout. There's not a finer bunch of people to break bread and fry fresh trout with.

BERNARDIED BROOKIES

Serves 3–4

12 brook trout, pan dressed
4 tablespoons butter
4 tablespoons concentrated orange juice
¼ medium onion, coarsely chopped
3 tablespoons bourbon
½ orange, thinly sliced

Arrange trout in a layer in 8-inch square baking dish with thickest parts of fish facing the outside of the dish.

In a small saucepan, micro butter and concentrated orange juice 1 minute on high.

Stir onions and bourbon into butter mixture. Pour this over the trout. Cover. Micro on 80 percent power for 5 minutes. Remove cover and spread orange slices over the top of the fish. Re-cover. Micro on 80 percent power for 5 minutes more.

Let sit for several minutes before serving to continue cooking.

Note: The origin of this recipe is a drink fondly called the Hot Bernardi. To those who've shared the Hot Bernardi, I hope you'll forgive the change in ingredients. Hot Bernardis are especially good after fishing for brook trout in your favorite neck of the woods.

BAKED ORANGE TROUT

Serves 4–6

1 5-pound trout
3 tablespoons mayonnaise
1 orange, unpeeled and sliced
1 onion, sliced

Place the fish in a large glass baking dish. Slather mayonnaise on the inside of the cavity and on the outside of the fish. Shield the head and the tail of the fish with small pieces of aluminum foil. Make sure pieces of foil are at least 1 inch from oven walls.

Lay the sliced orange and onion on the inside of the fish. Use toothpicks to close the cavity of the fish. Insert the temperature probe into the thickest part of the fish. Cover loosely with plastic wrap. Micro on 60 percent or bake until the temperature reaches 170 degrees, until the thickest part of the fish barely flakes.

Serve with tartar sauce or melted butter.

Note: This is great on cutthroat or lake trout. You may have to cut off the head and/or tail of the fish before it'll fit in your microwave.

Walleye and Pike

Many people mistakenly refer to walleyes as wall-eyed pike, when in fact the walleye is a member of the perch family. As such walleye are as good tasting as perch. In fact, many anglers feel the walleye is the best tasting fish of any family.

Because of the popularity of walleyes in the north-central states as well as Canada, they have also been stocked in many waters along the eastern seaboard and on into the West. A hybrid of walleyes was also stocked in some of these areas where walleyes are not native.

In Nevada, even though the populations of walleyes are small, the fish are of quite good size. For instance, the state record for walleye in the Silver State is over 13 pounds, a trophy fish in anyone's eyes.

Walleyes are a little different to fish for since they have habits unlike most other game fish. Walleyes, for one thing, are nocturnal fish. Due to unusual characteristics of their eyes, they are able to see at night, unlike most other fish species. This also enables them to see in murky waters.

The best times to fish for walleyes are in the early spring and fall when bait fish are not abundant. Right before a storm is also an excellent time to fish for them since the decrease in available light triggers the feeding pattern.

Northern pike and muskies, although with a much smaller range than the walleye, are popular with north-central fishermen and Canadian anglers. There are also small pockets of stocked pike that have done well in western waters. There are several pike fisheries in Nevada that provide out-of-the-ordinary fishing.

No matter what part of the country you live in, you'll probably live within range of one of three of the fish. Although muskies probably aren't caught as often as pike and fewer pike are probably taken than walleyes, they can all be used interchangeably in recipes, if you wish. Of course you'll have to make allowances for the different sizes of the fish.

Smaller fish can be baked whole, but if your fish is larger than five pounds, you'll probably be better off to fillet it. No matter which recipes you try, I'm sure you'll enjoy these fish very much for their excellent flavor—especially the mild flavored walleye.

PIKE WITH CREAMED SHRIMP SAUCE
Serves 3–4

   1½ *pounds pike fillets*
       Salt, to taste
       Freshly ground black pepper, to taste
   ¾ *cup milk*
   4 *tablespoons butter*
   2 *tablespoons flour*
   4 *tablespoons dry white wine*
   ¾ *cup light cream*
   ⅔ *cup cooked shrimp*
   1 *teaspoon lemon juice*
   ½ *teaspoon fennel seeds*

Place fillets in glass baking dish large enough to hold them in a single layer. Dust with salt and pepper. Pour milk over the top of the fish and dot with 2 tablespoons butter. Cover tightly. Poach fish for 5–8 minutes on 80 percent or reheat until fish barely flakes.

Drain the fish, reserving the liquid, and place the fish on a serving platter. Cover with aluminum foil, shiny side down.

In medium saucepan, micro 2 tablespoons butter on high for 1 minute. Stir in flour. Stir in cooking liquid and wine. Micro on 80 percent for 2–3 minutes or until thickened. Stir in cream, shrimp, lemon juice, and fennel. Micro on 80 percent or reheat for 2 minutes. Spoon the sauce over the fish.

WALLEYE PROVENCAL

Serves 3–4

1½ pounds walleye fillets
2½ tablespoons butter
1 cup mushrooms, sliced
½ medium onion, chopped
½ clove garlic, minced
1 tablespoon fresh parsley, chopped
1 cup canned peeled tomatoes, chopped
½ cup dry white wine

Micro butter in medium saucepan for 1 minute on high. Add mushrooms and micro on high for 3 minutes.

Arrange the fillets in a baking dish. Sprinkle with the mushrooms, onion, garlic, parsley, tomatoes, and wine.

Cover tightly. Micro on 80 percent for 6–9 minutes or until fish just barely flakes.

SPICY WALLEYE

Serves 3–4

1½–2 pounds walleye fillets
4 tablespoons butter
1 small onion, chopped
1 teaspoon chopped parsley
1 tablespoon flour
4 tablespoons water
1 bay leaf
Pinch of cinnamon
3 tablespoons dry white wine

In an 8-inch baking dish, micro butter on high for 1 minute. Add onion and parsley and micro on high for 3–4 minutes. Add the fillets on top of the onions. Cover and micro on 70 percent or roast for 5 minutes.

Combine flour and a little water to mix. Stir in bay leaf and cinnamon. Pour over the fish and cover. Micro on 70 percent for 3–6 minutes or until the center of the fish flakes easily.

Stir in wine and transfer to a warm serving platter.

HERBED PIKE
Serves 5–6

1 pike, 5–6 pounds, drawn
½ cup plus 2 teaspoons butter
1 tablespoon parsley, minced
⅛ teaspoon thyme
⅛ teaspoon marjoram
1 clove garlic, minced
½ cup dry white wine
2 teaspoons flour

Clean and scale the fish. Dot the inside with 6 tablespoons of the butter and sprinkle inside of the body with parsley, thyme, marjoram, and garlic. Close cavity with toothpicks.

Dot the top of the fish with 2 tablespoons of the butter. Insert the temperature probe into the thickest part of the fish. Cover loosely. Micro on 70 percent or roast until the temperature reaches 170 degrees, until the thickest part of the fish barely flakes. Baste with white wine every few minutes.

Move the fish to a serving platter. Cover with foil, shiny side down, while making sauce.

In a small bowl, cream together the 2 teaspoons of butter and the flour. Stir into pan juices. Micro on high for 2–3 minutes or until thickened. Season as desired and serve over the fish.

Fish from the Deep

Flounder

    The first time I caught flounder while bottom fishing in the San Pablo Bay in northern California, we filleted them and I brought them back the same day to my home in Reno. The next day, I sautéed the fillets and, man oh man, was I impressed with the difference between fresh flounder and fresh-frozen flounder or flounder that has sat around in the grocery store for several days after being transported. The difference is incredible. These fillets are some of the best fish I've ever tasted in my life.

When my father was a youngster he fished for flounder along the New York coast. When the tides were high, he fished for flounder off the jetties and when the tides were low, the quarry was mussels.

Flounder are easily obtained in fish markets and even in grocery stores. And while they are not usually treated in fish and game cookbooks, they certainly deserve a place of honor.

They are often the sole quarry of saltwater bottom anglers, but what is even more common is they're taken while fishing for other bottomfeeding species.

Since the fillets are quite often small, you should be careful not to overcook flounder. They can be steamed or sautéed effectively in the microwave and it doesn't take a lot of time to prepare them. Here, the key is simplicity. For the best flavor, they should be cooked in a little butter and served with even a little bit more.

Next time you find yourself with flounder in your catch, try these recipes and see if you aren't impressed with the flavor of fresh flounder fillets.

LEMON FLOUNDER
Serves 4

4 flounder fillets
4 tablespoons butter
2 teaspoons cornstarch
2 tablespoons water
½ cup fresh lemon juice
2 tablespoons honey
Lemon wedges
Parsley sprigs

Place butter in a glass baking dish large enough to hold the fillets in a single layer. Micro on high 1 minute. Place fillets on top of the melted butter. Cover tightly. Micro on 70 percent or roast for 5–8 minutes until fish just barely flakes.

Remove from oven and cover with foil, shiny side down, while making sauce.

In a medium saucepan, stir together cornstarch and water until smooth. Stir in lemon juice and honey. Micro on 80 percent or roast for 3–4 minutes until thickened.

Pour sauce over fillets and garnish with lemon wedges and parsley sprigs.

STUFFED FLOUNDER

Serves 4

4 flounders, 1 pound each
3 tablespoons butter
1 tablespoon bell pepper, chopped
3 tablespoons onion, chopped
¾ cup canned or fresh crabmeat
½ teaspoon parsley, chopped
Salt, to taste
Freshly ground black pepper, to taste
2 teaspoons lemon juice
Tabasco sauce, to taste

In a saucepan, micro butter for 1 minute on high. Add the bell pepper and onion. Micro on high for 1 minute. Add crabmeat, parsley, salt, pepper, lemon juice, and Tabasco.

Stuff the flounder loosely with mixture. Close with toothpicks. Arrange in a large baking dish and cover loosely. Micro on 70 percent for 12–15 minutes or until the thickest part of the fish barely flakes. Remove from oven and cover with foil for 3–5 minutes before serving. Remove the toothpicks.

Serve with melted butter.

Halibut

The first time I ever ate halibut, it was served in a rich, cheesy sauce that tasted wonderful. I've never been able to duplicate that same exact dish, but I found one to include in this cookbook that is very similar.

There are probably very few of us anglers who get to fish for halibut, so we've probably only eaten halibut that is at least a couple of days old. I like my fish a little fresher than that, but I'm satisfied with the fish my market usually carries.

The best part about this section is that there are a few new recipes you can use when you wish to serve fish and don't have anything in your own larder. Halibut is easy to find.

Although I've never fished for halibut, it is certainly one kind of fish I'd like to catch sometime. I've always thought catching big fish was really exciting and halibut certainly fits in the "large fish" category. I've seen films of people who have hooked into big halibut and they look like exciting fish to catch. Not only is it exciting hauling in a halibut, but the delicious meals you can prepare with this noble fish make the fight worthwhile.

The meat that comes from the halibut, usually steaked, is delicately flavored white meat that goes well with any number of sauces or butters.

Halibut makes a great entree to serve to guests. Everyone who likes fish will like halibut. The steaks are very handsome when presented with any number of garnishes. The meat is firm, if the fish is fresh, and shouldn't smell fishy. One large steak is really too big for one person, so you could cut the steaks into serving pieces before cooking, but this changes the visual appeal somewhat.

Halibut steaks can be poached or steamed and served with herbal butters or sauces (see my recipes in the section Sauces, Butters, and Marinades). It can also be baked in sauces in the microwave.

While halibut is probably not the most popular catch in the sea for the sportfisherman, halibut is one of the most popular fish at the checkout stand in the grocery store and fish market due to its wide availability.

Many fish recipes developed for conventional cooking methods will convert easily to microwave cooking. Make certain not to overcook the fish because it tends to get tough and dry if overcooked.

HALIBUT IN CHEESE SAUCE
Serves 2–3

1 large halibut steak
3 tablespoons butter
4 tablespoons flour
Salt, to taste
Freshly ground black pepper, to taste
¼ teaspoon nutmeg
1 cup milk
1 cup grated cheddar cheese
Paprika

Place steak in an 8-inch square baking dish.

In medium saucepan, micro butter 1 minute on high. Stir in flour, salt, pepper, and nutmeg. Gradually stir in milk.

Micro sauce on 80 percent or reheat for 3–5 minutes until thick, stirring once or twice. Add cheese, stirring until melted.

Pour sauce over fish. Cover loosely. Micro on 70 percent or roast for 15–18 minutes until fish barely flakes. Remove from oven and cover with foil, shiny side down, for 5 minutes before serving.

Sprinkle with paprika before serving.

HALIBUT ALMONDINE
Serves 2–4

  1 large (1½–2 pounds) halibut steak
    Salt, to taste
    Freshly ground black pepper, to taste
  ¼ cup butter
  ¼ cup slivered almonds, toasted
  2 teaspoons lemon juice
    Paprika
    Parsley sprigs
    Lemon slices

Place halibut steaks in 8-inch square baking dish (or one large enough to hold the steak). Sprinkle with salt and pepper.

In small saucepan, micro butter 1 minute on high. Add the toasted almonds and micro on 20 percent for 2 minutes. Pour butter and almonds over fish. Sprinkle fish with paprika.

Cover loosely. Micro on 70 percent or roast for 15–18 minutes until fish barely flakes. Remove from oven and cover with foil for 2–3 minutes. Garnish with parsley sprigs and lemon slices.

HALIBUT STEAKS WITH SESAME SEEDS
Serves 4

  2 halibut steaks
    Salt, to taste
    Freshly ground black pepper, to taste
  4 tablespoons butter
  3 tablespoons sesame seeds, toasted
  ¼ teaspoon tarragon
  1 teaspoon lemon juice
    Lemon slices

Arrange halibut steaks in a glass baking dish large enough to hold them. Sprinkle with salt and pepper.

Micro butter, in small saucepan, 1 minute on high. Stir in sesame seeds, tarragon, and lemon juice. Sprinkle the mixture over the steaks. Cover loosely.

Micro on 70 percent or roast for 18–20 minutes until fish barely flakes. Remove from oven and cover with foil, shiny side down, for 2–3 minutes before serving. Garnish with lemon slices.

Sturgeon

There have been a lot of stories written about these prehistoric-looking fish. Sturgeon are popular catches in many areas, such as the San Francisco Bay area and tributaries leading to the bay.

Many of the stories surrounding sturgeon are of huge, so-called "sea monsters" often sighted in freshwater lakes. Although many of the accounts of sightings of the sea monsters are not documented, biologists believe that sturgeon, which grow to immense proportions, were once released into these lakes. Just recently a California lake was drained and a six-foot-long sturgeon was found. This old guy had caused plenty of "big fish" stories. In old records on the lake, several releases of sturgeon were documented.

I fished for sturgeon a couple of years ago in the San Pablo Bay near Sausalito, California. It was a tense day of bottom fishing, watching for the slight tap, tap, tap on the rod tip. Finally, when I patiently had been fishing without success for several hours, I had a bite that was different from the rays and the flounder we'd been catching.

I immediately set the hook. The fish dove straight down, pumping as he went. He felt like a good fish. He fought like no other fish I'd ever caught before. When we finally got him to the boat, we lifted him aboard for the measurements. In California, a keeper had to be at least 40 inches. He barely squeaked by at 43 inches, but he was a keeper. I was the only one to catch a keeper that day.

I was not enamored of that fish. He was ugly, with a sucker mouth on the underside of his body. A certain throwback to his prehistoric cousins. I couldn't imagine that any fish that ugly could taste so good.

I steaked the fish and also smoked some of the meat. It was really good, although I had to make certain to remove any brown or gray colored meat and cut off any fat from him. These areas don't taste good and can ruin the taste of the rest of the meat if not removed.

If overcooked, sturgeon can become very rubbery, so be careful when you microwave it.

I have never found recipes anywhere for sturgeon, so I developed a couple here for those sturgeon fishermen who bring back keepers. The recipe for Market Street Sturgeon was developed after tasting sturgeon prepared similarly at a fish feed held by Ed Ow, the former publisher of *Angler* magazine.

MARKET STREET STURGEON STEAKS
Serves 4

4 large sturgeon steaks or 8 small steaks
½ lemon cut in slices
1 tablespoon white vinegar
2 peppercorns
1 cup hot water

Sauce:

1 cup milk
2 tablespoons butter
2 tablespoons flour
¼ teaspoon white pepper
2 tablespoons capers
 Salt, to taste
 Fresh dill
 Lemon wedges

Combine lemon slices, white vinegar, peppercorns, and hot water. Microwave on high 5 minutes. Add sturgeon steaks. Cover with plastic wrap. Micro on high 2–3 minutes.

Remove from oven and cover with aluminum foil shiny side down while making sauce.

Sauce: In small bowl, heat milk on 70 percent power or roast setting for 2 minutes. Set aside.

In small bowl, melt butter on high 1 minute. Stir in flour. Cook on high 1 minute. Stir in milk, pepper, and capers. Cook on high 3–4 minutes, until boiling. Stir once during cooking time.

Arrange sturgeon steaks on serving platter. Pour sauce over steaks. Garnish with fresh dill and lemon wedges.

SPICY TOMATO STURGEON STEAKS
Serves 4

4 sturgeon steaks
2 medium onions, chopped
3 cloves garlic, minced
2 tablespoons olive oil
2 large tomatoes, chopped coarsely
1 teaspoon basil
¼ cup fresh parsley, minced
½ cup dry white wine

Combine onions, garlic, and olive oil in microwave saucepan. Cover and micro on high 5–6 minutes.

Add tomatoes, basil, parsley, and wine. Cover and micro on high until boiling (about 7–9 minutes).

Arrange fish steaks in baking dish just large enough to hold them with the thin parts in the center of the dish. Pour sauce over top of steaks.

Microwave on high 7–8 minutes, turning the fillets over halfway through cooking. Remove from oven and cover with aluminum shiny side down for 2–3 minutes to finish cooking.

Note: Sturgeon doesn't flake in the way many fish do, so the flaking test won't work. Be careful, though, not to overcook as sturgeon tends to get rubbery if overcooked.

Appetizers

Appetizers are served prior to a meal or as finger foods at parties. Imagine the delight of your guests when you serve innovative appetizers made with fish and game. Not only will your guests at your annual game feed enjoy these foods, but I'll bet you can entice some non-game eaters into trying this new fare, especially when they're not faced with a whole meal of it.

You'll really appreciate your microwave oven when it comes to preparing hot appetizers. You won't spend all your time in the kitchen preparing them in your oven and your guests won't be forced to eat cold, stale food. Never again will you have to worry about your guests being late. Everything will be fresh when you take it out of the microwave after only a few short minutes.

My family and guests are used to finding fish and game turn up in some pretty unique foods. We eat so much fish and game, it's a challenge to come up with new recipes including them. One way to surprise your family is to make some hors d'oeuvres and serve them before dinner some night—a makeshift cocktail hour. They'll appreciate something new in their schedules and it'll give your family more time to spend together.

Guests at a game feed are expecting the new and different. If you have recipes you'd like to try on the crowd, a game feed is one of the easiest ways to do it.

Many of your own recipes for your favorite appetizers can be altered to allow the use of fish or game. In recipes using sausage, just use some of the game sausage you've got stashed in the freezer. If you don't usually have some sausage or salami made up from your game, you're missing some good eating. You should ask your game processor to let you taste a sample of the salami or sausage they make. Processors use different recipes and it may take a while to find a recipe you like. Or maybe you ought to try making your own sausage. Many game cookbooks feature recipes for game sausage.

Often recipes with a cream cheese or sour cream base will benefit from adding cooked or smoked salmon. You can substitute salmon for clams in a dip, either hot or cold.

When you cook canapes in the microwave, it is best to cook half a batch at a time. Most canapes can be prepared ahead of serving time and refrigerated or frozen. It only takes a few minutes in the microwave to bring them to serving temperature.

Be careful when you judge the times for cooking appetizers. Hot dips made of sour cream or cream cheese should be warmed slowly, so you won't want to cook them at a high setting. Appetizers with oily or fatty bases, such as oily fish or recipes with sausage, mayonnaise, or butter, take less time to cook. Sometimes the ingredients in appetizers will pop or burst in the microwave so it may help to lightly cover your appetizers when you put them in the oven or you'll spend a lot of time cleaning the inside of your microwave. It helps to lower the power setting on appetizers that may pop.

Appetizers are a great way to dispense of leftovers. Leftover cooked salmon is a great ingredient as are other types of cooked fish. Use your imagination when it comes to new recipes for your leftovers. When you use your microwave, no one will ever know you're serving leftovers.

Remember not to serve too many appetizers to your guests. The idea isn't to fill them up, but to help stimulate their appetites.

MARINATED MUSHROOMS
20–30 appetizers

⅔ cup olive oil
½ cup water
Juice of 2 lemons
1 bay leaf
2 garlic cloves, cut in half
6 peppercorns
½ teaspoon salt
1 pound small fresh mushrooms

Combine all the ingredients except mushrooms in a glass casserole dish. Cover. Microwave on high 5 minutes or until boiling. Micro 5 minutes more on medium (simmer or 50 percent power) setting.

Add mushrooms. Stir until well coated. Cover. Micro on high 2 minutes. Stir. Re-cover. Micro on high 3 minutes more. Let mushrooms cool in marinade. Refrigerate overnight.

The mushrooms should be served cool. It's best to allow them to drain or pat them dry with toweling before serving. Serve on a traditional antipasto platter or alone with wine and cheese.

JOE GREEN'S CHUKAR BITS
36 appetizers

12 slices bacon
8 ounces chukar meat, cut in small chunks
¼ teaspoon garlic powder
¼ cup soy sauce

Cut bacon into thirds. Mix garlic powder in soy sauce. Dip chukar pieces in soy sauce. Wrap in ⅓ slice bacon.

Secure with wooden toothpicks. Place 12 at a time on a paper towel–lined plate. Cover with paper towels.

Micro on high 4–5 minutes or until bacon is crisp.

CREAMY SALMON DIP
Serves 15–20

1 round loaf French bread
2 cups sour cream
2 8-ounce packages cream cheese
1 cup smoked salmon, flaked
½ medium onion, chopped finely
1 green pepper, chopped finely
Chopped parsley
Carrot sticks
Celery sticks

Cut top off French bread. Hollow bread out of inside. Save the removed bread. Set the outside bread crust aside.

Cut remaining bread into cubes. Place on plate, uncovered. Micro on high 1–2 minutes to dry. Set aside to use as dippers. Mix sour cream, cream cheese, salmon, onion, and green pepper. Pour into hollowed out French bread. Place on microproof plate. Cover loosely. Micro on high 4 minutes. Stir well. Micro on high 4 minutes more.

Preheat conventional oven to bake 250 degrees. Place in conventional oven. Bake at 250 degrees for 1 hour. Garnish with parsley.

Serve with carrot sticks, celery sticks, and dried bread cubes for dippers.

Note: When dip is gone, break bread crust into bite-sized pieces and eat. This is delicious. I guarantee it will blow anyone's diet.

SAUSAGE BALLS

Approximately 80 hors d'oeuvres

2 cups Bisquick
2 cups sharp cheddar cheese
1 pound game sausage (I like antelope)
2 tablespoons onion, diced
1 tablespoon poultry seasoning

Combine ingredients and shape into small balls, about the diameter of a quarter. Place them on a bacon rack or on a pie pan. Micro 8 balls at a time on 50 percent or simmer for 4–5 minutes until sausage is well cooked.

Allow the sausage balls to sit a few minutes before removing them from their baking dish.

Note: Sometimes the balls get a little flattened out and they might not be super attractive, but they are delicious. They can be made ahead and refrigerated before cooking. I like to bring them to room temperature before microwaving, though, or they tend to crumble.

HOT SALMON DIP

Approximately 2 cups

1 8-ounce package cream cheese
1 tablespoon milk
1 teaspoon Worcestershire sauce
½ cup smoked salmon
2 tablespoons chives, chopped
⅛ teaspoon onion salt
   Pinch of cayenne pepper

Blend cream cheese, milk, and Worcestershire sauce with electric mixer in small bowl.

Stir in the remaining ingredients. Pour into 1-quart casserole.

Micro on 60 percent or bake for 4–5 minutes until warm.

Serve as a dip with fresh veggies or crackers.

HOT FISH CANAPES
25 canapes

½ cup cooked bass or walleye
1 cup mayonnaise
1 teaspoon lime juice
   Freshly ground black pepper
1 egg white
   Crackers

Blend fish, mayonnaise, lime juice, and pepper in a small bowl.
Beat egg white with mixer until stiff. Fold into fish mixture.
Spoon approximately 1 teaspoon of fish mixture on each cracker. Place half of the canapes on a microproof serving dish.
Micro on high 1–2 minutes or until heated through. Repeat with the remaining canapes until finished. Serve hot.

ANTELOPE SAUSAGE CANAPES
16 appetizers

½ pound antelope sausage
¼ cup sour cream
1 tablespoon horseradish
2 tablespoons chives
   Dash cayenne pepper
16 slices of small cocktail rye bread, toasted
   Paprika

Place sausage in 1-quart casserole. Micro on high for 2–3 minutes or until done, stirring once or twice to break up pieces. Drain well.
Stir in sour cream, horseradish, chives, and pepper.
Spread sausage mixture on rye toast. Sprinkle with paprika. Arrange half of them on a plate lined with paper toweling.
Micro on high 1 minute or until heated through. Repeat with remaining canapes.

STUFFED MUSHROOMS
24–30 appetizers

1 pound large fresh mushrooms
¼ pound game sausage (antelope, venison, elk)
1 clove garlic, minced
¼ cup onion, minced
1 tablespoon fresh parsley, minced
1 teaspoon Kitchen Bouquet
¼ cup sour cream
2 tablespoons Parmesan cheese

Remove stems from mushrooms. Set aside.

Combine sausage, garlic, onion, parsley, and Kitchen Bouquet and stir well. Micro on high for 4–5 minutes or until sausage is cooked (not overcooked, though). Stir in sour cream and cheese.

Fill each mushroom with sausage mixture. Arrange 10–12 mushrooms on a plate. Micro on 70 percent power or roast for 3–5 minutes until heated through. Repeat with remaining mushrooms.

SWEDISH MEATBALLS
24–30 meatballs

1 pound ground elk or venison
½ pound game sausage (antelope, elk, or venison)
½ medium onion, chopped
¾ cup dry bread crumbs
½ teaspoon freshly ground black pepper
1 teaspoon Worcestershire sauce
1 egg
¼ cup milk
¼ cup oil
¼ cup flour
1 teaspoon paprika
Salt and pepper, to taste
1 cup water
¾ cup sour cream

Mix ground meat, sausage, onion, bread crumbs, pepper, Worcestershire sauce, egg, and milk. Stir well. Refrigerate 2–3 hours.

Blend oil, flour, paprika, salt and pepper to taste in 2-quart casserole. Micro on 50 percent 2–3 minutes. Stir in water. Micro on high 3–4 minutes or until boiling. Allow to boil 1 minute. Stir well. Stir in sour cream, mixing until smooth.

Roll meat mixture into balls about 1 inch in diameter. Brown the meatballs lightly in skillet or microwave browning dish. Place meat in sauce. Spoon sauce over meatballs. Micro on high 7 minutes or until meat is cooked. Stir meatballs gently halfway through cooking time.

Serve with toothpicks.

CHEESE AND FISH DIP
Serves 6–8

1 8-ounce Gouda cheese
1 tablespoon milk
1 tablespoon sherry
2 tablespoons cooked, flaked fish (walleye, bass, or panfish)
1 teaspoon prepared mustard
  Tabasco sauce, to taste
  Paprika

Unwrap the cheese and soften in microwave on 10 percent or low power for 30–45 seconds until softened. Make petals in the cheese by making four intersecting cuts in the top and curling each section as you pull it back.

Scoop out the cheese, but leave a thin wall as a shell. Refrigerate shell.

Mash cheese with a fork and blend in milk, sherry, fish, mustard, and Tabasco.

Fill shell with mixture. Cover and refrigerate for 3–4 hours. Soften at room temperature or on low in the microwave before serving. Sprinkle with paprika, if desired.

ARTICHOKE HEARTS
Serves 4

4 artichoke hearts
1 tablespoon butter
4 hard rolls
¾ cup mozzarella cheese
1 egg
2 tablespoons milk
  Salt and pepper, to taste

Combine artichoke hearts and butter in a small saucepan. Micro on high 2 minutes.

Cut the top off the rolls and scoop out the inside bread. Place one artichoke heart in each roll.

Mix the cheese, egg, milk, salt, and pepper. Spoon the mixture over the artichoke hearts in each roll.

Place the rolls on a glass dish. Micro on 60 percent or bake for 4–5 minutes until heated through.

Serve Alongs

Fish and game entrees provide excellent meals. One of the problems I've always found is preparing side dishes or desserts that go well with game. Of course there are the traditional favorites.

No self-respecting game cookbook author would leave out a recipe for a traditional dish such as wild rice. This book will not be an exception to this rule. Wild rice is quick, delicious, and firm when cooked in the microwave. It reduces your cooking time to almost nothing.

Since microwaves do such a nice job on vegetables, you'll find recipes for many of my favorites in this section. You'll like the one for candied carrots and will want to serve it often.

I like the way the microwave does baked goods. One of my favorite recipes in the whole book is the one for Mexican cornbread. It is far different than most traditional cornbreads because it's light and very, very moist. It's superb served with your favorite fish dishes.

Because the baked goods come out so nicely, I decided to convert some of my favorite sourdough recipes for use in the microwave. The blueberry muffins are also delicious and although they're traditionally served at breakfast, I'd serve them along with some of the recipes for salads or for waterfowl. They're so good, no one will complain *when* you serve them, only when you don't.

Some of the recipes don't need a microwave or any oven to prepare. I hope you don't mind that I sneaked them in. I couldn't resist including some of my favorite recipes that go well with game. Most of them don't need any cooking. I hope you enjoy them, because they go extremely well with both fish and game dishes.

When deciding which dishes to serve with game—well, there aren't any rules, so use your imagination. Of course some dishes complement fish better and some complement game better. I've never had wild rice served with fish, but that's not to say it wouldn't be good.

One of the things I keep in mind when preparing a dish is what the accompaniments will look like. Many of the dishes in this book have sauces attached to them since cooking that way is so successful in the microwave. Keep in mind what the ingredients of the recipe will look like. For instance, with tomato dishes, I like to serve something contrasting in color so I'll often serve a green vegetable.

I also strive for a balance of tastes. If the flavor is very spicy in the entree, I switch to something with a bland flavor as a side dish. If you're serving a heavy soup or stew, serve a light, crispy salad as an accompaniment. That way you won't drown out the flavors. The key is to accent the flavors, not hide them or mask them.

Visual appeal is as important to a meal as the taste of the food in my opinion. The side dishes work with the entree to create an ambiance. Be creative in your choices.

There are some traditional side dishes such as hush puppies that you won't find here. While I enjoy cooking in the microwave, it doesn't do everything and I haven't discovered a method of cooking the hush puppies in any method other than the traditional one.

Most of the recipes that need cooking can be whipped up in the microwave during those last few minutes when your entree comes out of the oven and sits to finish cooking.

If you have a large microwave, you might want to consider cooking a complete meal at once. You'll have to adjust your times though, adding more time to allow everything to cook through. Even though I have a large microwave with a rack included, I rarely use it, preferring to add the dishes to the oven at the end. It seems like you save time doing it in that manner.

MARINATED CUCUMBER SALAD

Serves 4

3 cucumbers, shredded finely
1 cup white vinegar
4 tablespoons sugar
Carrot shreds

Mix all the ingredients. Chill for 10–12 hours before serving.
Drain the marinated cucumbers thoroughly before serving. Garnish with a few shreds of carrot.

AUNT ROSE AND NETTIE'S OLIVE AND CELERY SALAD

Serves 8–10

2 cups pitted Spanish or Italian-style green olives
3 cups celery, sliced
⅓ cup olive oil
1 cup white vinegar
⅛–¼ teaspoon ground red pepper to taste, or 3–4 chili tepines, crushed
1 teaspoon oregano

Mix all ingredients. Marinade overnight, stirring a couple of times during that time. Strain before serving.

Note: My paternal grandmother used to serve this dish. But she died shortly after I was born so I never knew her. My Aunt Rose and Aunt Nettie in the Bronx, New York, have passed on some of the recipes of our family, whose origins are Calabria, Italy. This salad is one of those recipes. Although it doesn't sound that appetizing, it really is very good.

To easily pit the olives, hit them on the side with a mallet. My grandmother used to crack the pits to allow the oils of the olive pit to mix with the salad for improved taste, but it's much easier to remove the pits initially. *Buon appetito, con gusto!*

HOT SPINACH SALAD

Serves 10

5 strips bacon
2 eggs, hard-cooked and chopped
1½ pounds spinach
2 cups mushrooms, sliced
1 clove garlic, minced
¾ cup cooking oil
½ cup red wine vinegar
Freshly ground black pepper
Croutons

Place bacon strips on bacon rack. Micro on high 5 minutes. Allow to cool. Crumble. Combine bacon, eggs, spinach, and mushrooms. Chill for 2–3 hours.

Combine garlic, oil, vinegar, and pepper. Micro on low or 20 percent for 5 minutes until hot.

Pour dressing over spinach. Toss well. Garnish with croutons, if desired.

Note: This is a very colorful salad that goes well with either fish or game. I serve it with elk steaks most often. There's plenty here for company.

SAUERKRAUT SALAD

Serves 6–8

1 27-ounce can sauerkraut
1 cup celery, chopped
1 cup carrots, chopped
1 cup green peppers, chopped
1 cup red onions, chopped
⅓ cup vinegar
⅓ cup oil
1 cup sugar

Drain, rinse, and squeeze sauerkraut to remove liquid. Mix sauerkraut, celery, carrots, green peppers, and red onions.

In a small saucepan, mix vinegar and oil. Micro on high 2 minutes. Stir in sugar. Allow to cool.

Pour the vinegar, oil, and sugar mix over the sauerkraut mixture. Refrigerate overnight. Stir once or twice during refrigeration time.

ASPARAGUS VINAIGRETTE

Serves 6–8

1 pound asparagus
1 tablespoon olive oil
1 tablespoon white vinegar
2 tablespoons lemon juice
1 teaspoon Dijon mustard
¼ teaspoon rosemary

Trim woody ends off asparagus stalks. Lay flat on microproof baking dish or plate. Add 2–3 tablespoons water. Cover tightly with plastic wrap.

Mix remaining ingredients in small saucepan. Place both asparagus and the vinaigrette in microwave. Microwave on high for 3–4 minutes.

Remove both from oven. Combine both in serving bowl, toss to cover asparagus completely with vinaigrette.

Note: Asparagus is excellent cooked in the microwave. It retains its color and texture.

CARAWAY SLAW

Serves 6

1 large head cabbage, shredded
1 small onion, chopped finely
Salt, if desired
Ground pepper, to taste
3 tablespoons lemon juice
1 tablespoon sugar
¾ cup mayonnaise
1 tablespoon caraway seeds
1 tablespoon cider vinegar

Combine all ingredients in a large bowl. Stir thoroughly. Adjust seasonings to taste. Chill 3–4 hours before serving.

GLAZED CARROTS AND PEAS
Serves 4–6

2 cups frozen baby carrots, thawed
1 cup frozen peas, thawed
¼ cup brown sugar
3 tablespoons butter
⅛ teaspoon nutmeg

In a 1-quart casserole, mix carrots and peas. Set aside.

In a small saucepan, combine brown sugar, butter, and nutmeg. Micro on high 1 minute. Stir.

Pour brown sugar mixture over carrots and peas. Stir well. Micro on high 5–7 minutes, stirring once while cooking. Drain before serving.

Note: This is a brightly colored dish that goes well with either fish or game.

MAGIC CORN ON THE COB
Serves 4

4 ears corn, in husks
Salt and freshly ground pepper
Butter

Soak corn, still in the husks, in water for at least 5 minutes. Wrap individually in waxed paper.

Micro on high for 12 minutes, turning once during cooking time.

Remove the husks and dust with salt and pepper. Serve with ample supplies of butter.

Note: This is quick and just terrific for corn.

BUTTERNUTTY SQUASH
Serves 2

1 butternut squash
4 tablespoons butter
3 tablespoons brown sugar, packed
3 tablespoons walnuts, chopped
3 tablespoons raisins
Nutmeg

Cut the butternut squash in half lengthwise. Hollow out the seeds and pulp area. Place cut side down in glass baking dish.

Place butter in small dish and microwave on high for 1 minute to melt. Set aside.

Microwave squash on high for 8 minutes uncovered. Remove from the oven.

While the squash is cooking, mix the sugar, walnuts, and raisins in the melted butter. When squash is finished, remove it from oven and spoon the sugar mixture in the hollowed out section. Sprinkle the entire squash with nutmeg.

Microwave, uncovered, for 6–8 minutes until the meat is tender. Allow to sit for 2–3 minutes before serving.

KATHY CHILTON'S MEXICAN BEAN DIP
Serves 10–20

3½ cups pork and beans in tomato sauce
½ cup shredded sharp cheddar cheese
1 teaspoon garlic salt
1 teaspoon chili powder
½ teaspoon salt
2 teaspoons vinegar
2 teaspoons Worcestershire sauce
½ teaspoon liquid smoke
4 slices bacon, cooked and crumbled

Pour pork and beans in blender or food processor and blend until smooth. Pour into medium casserole and stir in remaining ingredients, except bacon.

Cover lightly. Micro on 70 percent or roast for 4–5 minutes until heated through. Sprinkle bacon on top and serve with corn chips.

HOT SALSA
Serves 10–20

    1 1-pound can whole tomatoes, drained and chopped
    1 4-ounce can green chilies, chopped
    ½ cup chopped green onions
    ½ teaspoon salt
    ½ teaspoon oregano
    1 teaspoon vinegar
    1 teaspoon olive oil

Mix all ingredients together. Cover loosely. Micro on high for 2–3 minutes or until heated through. Serve with corn chips.

DOROTHY'S CABBAGE CASSEROLE
Serves 6–8

    3 cups corn flakes, crushed
    1 cup cheddar cheese, grated
    1 head cabbage, shredded
    ⅓ cup water
    3 tablespoons butter
    ½ cup onion, chopped
    3 tablespoons flour
    1 teaspoon salt
      Pepper, to taste
    1 2-pound can whole tomatoes
    ⅓ cup green pepper, chopped

Mix the corn flakes and cheddar cheese and set aside.

Place the cabbage in a medium casserole. Pour the water over the cabbage and cover the dish. Microwave on high for 5 minutes. Drain.

In a medium saucepan, micro butter 1 minute on high. Add onions. Micro on high for 2 minutes. Stir in flour, salt, and pepper. Micro 1 minute on high.

Stir in tomatoes and green pepper. Micro on 70 percent for 4–5 minutes or until mixture thickens.

In a large casserole, spread a third of the tomato mixture, then half of the cabbage. Alternate rest of cabbage and tomato mixture. Cover the top with cornflake mixture.

Cover and micro on 60 percent or bake for 15 minutes until heated through.

SOUR CREAM POTATO CASSEROLE
Serves 8–10

1 2-pound bag frozen Southern-style or hash brown potatoes
¾ cup butter
1 medium onion, chopped
2 cans cream of chicken soup, undiluted
1 pint sour cream
½ teaspoon salt
2 cups Longhorn cheese, grated
2 cups corn flakes, crushed

Place a paper towel in your microwave. Place bag of frozen potatoes on the towel. Microwave on 30 percent or defrost for 15 minutes. Remove from the oven and let stand enclosed in bag until ready to mix with the other ingredients.

In a 4-quart bowl, microwave ½ cup of the butter for 1 minute on high. Stir in chopped onion and microwave on high for 4 minutes. Add soup, sour cream, salt, cheese, and potatoes. Mix well.

Divide ingredients into two 8-inch square glass casserole dishes. Melt ¼ cup of the butter and mix with corn flakes. Divide in two and place the crumbs upon the two dishes of potatoes.

Return each dish to microwave and cook until hot and bubbly, about 5–8 minutes on high.

Note: This dish is excellent when served with fish dishes or informal game dishes.

PARSLEY NEW POTATOES
Serves 4

    12 small new potatoes
    ¼ cup water
    1 tablespoon fresh parsley, minced
    3 tablespoons butter, melted
    1 clove garlic, sliced
       Freshly ground pepper, to taste
    1 tablespoon Parmesan chesse

Wash the potatoes well. Cut ½-inch strip around the middle of potatoes. Place the potatoes and water in a 2-quart casserole. Cover. Micro on high 10–12 minutes. Stir once during cooking. Drain.

Combine parsley, butter, garlic, pepper, and Parmesan cheese in a small bowl. Mix well. Pour over potatoes.

Note: This dish goes well with both fish and game, but I like it with delicate flavors in a fish dish.

NUTTY WILD RICE
Serves 4–6

    1 cup fancy wild rice
    2 cups water
    2 tablespoons butter
    ½ cup pecans, chopped
       Salt
       Freshly ground pepper

Rinse the wild rice thoroughly. Combine rice and water in a 1½-quart casserole. Microwave on high 6–7 minutes or until boiling. Stir.

Cover. Microwave 30 minutes on 50 percent or simmer setting. Remove from microwave and set aside.

Meanwhile, micro 2 tablespoons butter in small saucepan on high 1 minute. Add pecans. Micro on high two minutes.

Make certain rice absorbs all the water. If not, drain the rice well.

Pour butter and pecans over rice. Toss to coat. Add salt to taste, if desired. Add six or seven grindings of fresh pepper. Reheat, if desired, before serving.

Note: Buy only the real wild rice for just that right extra touch to your game recipes. I order mine from a company in Minnesota. Write: Voyageur Gift & Trading Company, Box 35121 Normandale Branch, Minneapolis, MN 55435.

MEXICAN CORNBREAD
Serves 6–8

1 cup yellow cornmeal
1 cup flour
1 teaspoon baking powder
1 teaspoon salt
1 egg
1 cup milk
1 cup cream-style corn
¼ cup onion, chopped
2 tablespoons green chilies, chopped
2 tablespoons pimientos, chopped
¼ cup butter
½ cup cheddar cheese, shredded

Combine dry ingredients in bowl and mix well. In another bowl beat egg and milk together. Stir in corn and set aside. Combine onion, chilies, and pimientos with butter in small saucepan. Micro on high 2 minutes.

Add milk mixture, onion mixture, and cheese to dry ingredients. Stir until just mixed. Pour into well-buttered glass ring or bundt pan.

Micro on simmer (medium or 50 percent power setting) 12 minutes. Turn pan. Cook on high 8–10 minutes or until toothpick comes out clean when inserted near the center. Remove from microwave and cover with aluminum foil, shiny side down, for 5 minutes to finish cooking.

Note: If you don't have a microproof ring or bundt pan, use a glass bowl, well-buttered, with a drinking glass in the center (open end facing up). Make certain to grease the bottom of the glass well, too. This recipe is one of my favorites. Occasionally, depending on the humidity in the air, the cornbread comes out a bit gooey in the center. To solve that, rather than cook it longer—the edges become tough if you do—I place individual pieces in the microwave a few minutes to warm.

SOURDOUGH BLUEBERRY MUFFINS

12 muffins

1 cup flour, sifted
1 teaspoon baking powder
⅓ cup sugar
½ teaspoon salt
1 egg yolk, slightly beaten
1 cup milk
1 cup sourdough starter
4 tablespoons shortening, melted
1 egg white, stiffly beaten
1 cup blueberries, fresh or frozen

Sift flour once, measure. Add baking powder, sugar, salt and sift again.
Combine egg yolk and milk. Add to flour mixture. Add sourdough starter. Add shortening. Mix only enough to dampen flour. Fold in egg white and blueberries.
Pour batter into paper baking cups or a microproof muffin pan. Micro 6 muffins at a time 4–5 minutes on bake or 60 percent until muffins are no longer doughy.

ORANGE PECAN MUFFINS

12–15 muffins

1 egg
1 cup milk
¼ cup salad oil
2 cups flour
¼ cup sugar
1½ teaspoons baking powder
1 teaspoon salt
1 tablespoon grated orange peel
¼ cup pecans, chopped

Beat egg, stir in milk and oil. Mix in remaining ingredients until just moistened.

Cook six at a time in microproof muffin pan (with or without paper cups) on 60 percent or bake setting 4–5 minutes until no longer doughy. I found it's not necessary to grease the muffin tin but you might want to use a non-stick spray to make sure.

Note: If these are overcooked, you might as well use them to practice your bat swing. If the first batch is overcooked, reduce the amount of time you use.

BLACKBERRY SOURDOUGH COBBLER
Serves 6

1 cup flour
1 teaspoon salt
6 tablespoons shortening
¾ cup sourdough starter
21-ounce can blackberry filling
Vanilla ice cream

Mix flour and salt in large glass bowl. Cut the shortening into the flour until it resembles coarse cornmeal. Stir in the starter with a large wooden spoon. Roll the dough into a ball. Roll the ball into a square approximately 12 × 12 inches. Line a 2-quart casserole or 8-inch square glass baking dish with the dough. Don't trim the edges. Spoon the filling into the lined dish.

Fold the crust edges over the top of the filling. Microwave on bake or 60 percent 15–20 minutes until crust is cooked, turning once to cook evenly.

Serve hot with a big scoop of vanilla ice cream.

Note: Some people don't like the pale look of the crust cooked in the microwave oven. If you'd like the top browned, after you take the cobbler out of the microwave brush the top with melted butter and place under the broiler of your conventional oven for a few minutes until brown.

AMARETTO STRAWBERRIES AND ICE CREAM
Serves 8–10

1 cup sugar
½ cup water
2 tablespoons cornstarch
2 cups strawberries, halved
3 tablespoons Amaretto liqueur
  Almond or French vanilla ice cream

Combine sugar, water, and cornstarch in microwave saucepan. Stir well to combine. Add strawberries.

Micro on high 3-5 minutes or until the mixture comes to a boil. Micro 2-3 minutes more or until thickened. Remove from oven. Add Amaretto. Stir well. Chill.

Serve over ice cream in parfait glasses.

Note: The colors of the berries tend to "wash out" after they're cooked, so I like to add one or two drops of red food coloring to perk up the looks of this great, light dessert.

THE BRAIDS CHOCOLATE BANANAS
Serves 4

4 bananas, peeled
¼ cup small chocolate chips
3 tablespoons graham cracker crumbs

Place bananas in medium-size baking dish. Slice halfway through the banana lengthwise.

Press chocolate chips into the banana.

Sprinkle with graham cracker crumbs. Cover loosely.

Micro on high 3-4 minutes or until chocolate is melted.

Note: The first time I had bananas cooked this way was during a shore lunch on the banks of the Alagnak River on the Alaskan Peninsula. The bananas remained in their peels and were wrapped in foil and stuffed into the hot coals. Kids and "chocoholics" love this recipe.

BAKED APPLES
Serves 2

2 large baking apples
2 teaspoons butter
4 teaspoons brown sugar
¼ teaspoon cinnamon
¼ teaspoon nutmeg
2 teaspoons raisins
1 tablespoon walnuts, chopped
2 tablespoons water

Core apples and make a slit in skin all around the middle to keep apples from bursting. Place apples in small baking dish.

In small bowl, melt butter on high 30 seconds. Stir in brown sugar, cinnamon, nutmeg, raisins, and walnuts. Fill each apple with mixture.

Add water to bottom of dish. Cover. Micro on high 4–5 minutes.

Sauces, Butters, And Marinades

This is one of my favorite sections of the whole book. Why? There's not even any fish or game included in any one of these recipes.

Well, we fish and game cooks spend so much of our time concocting recipes for thick masking flavors to cook fish or game in, especially game. We're so afraid of the meat tasting "gamey." Sauce it with heavy sauces and marinade it until it tastes like vinegar, then serve it and you probably still won't get good responses to your fish or game cooking.

The whole solution to the problem is to enhance the flavors of the fish or game, but not to hide them or disguise them or mask them. The whole solution is in very simple cooking. Often that is the very best treatment for fish and game.

There's probably nothing better than a steak cooked medium to medium-rare topped with an herbed butter or maybe a little crumbled bleu cheese. Nothing quite surpasses a fish fillet with a little lemon butter or perhaps some fresh tartar sauce.

Of course there are those times when your piece of meat isn't as perfect as you'd like to present for one reason or another. There seems to be little rhyme or reason for it. Some may say the age of the animal is the deciding factor, others say it's their forage food. Some say it is dependent on the conditions when you shot the deer. Nevertheless, I've had people tell me they've tasted meat from big, old mule deer that has been tastier than a young buck. So it's kind of a matter of the luck of the draw, plus the conditions mentioned above.

Here again, I'm convinced good field care is one of the big determining factors. But if you end up stuck with a piece of meat that is tough or too gamey tasting, a marinade from this section may save that piece of meat for you and I'm all for that.

There are also times when you want the dominant flavor of a marinade to take over the taste of the game. Some cooks marinade their game in water with salt and/or vinegar in it before cooking. Some cooks swear that you shouldn't touch water to the meat. Some soak their game meat in milk before cooking it. I can't say one method works better than another; you'll just have to experiment with the game meat you have to work with until you find what works best for your own taste buds and those of your family.

Once you start making sauces in the microwave, you'll never go back to conventional methods. I promise. First of all, it takes little time to bring the sauce to a boil. Even at a low power setting it only takes several minutes. Then once your sauce is boiling, it only takes a minute or two to completely thicken the sauce.

The best part about all this is that your sauce will not burn in the microwave since there's no direct heat. You'll have no problems making seemingly difficult bearnaise or hollandaise sauce in the microwave. Sauces you once shied away from are now simple in the microwave.

When it comes to making flavored butters for use on vegetables, fish, or meat, the microwave will also come in handy. You can use the low power setting or just a few seconds on high to soften the butter so it'll be easier to whip.

These herb flavored or colored butters make excellent garnishes. When you are serving dinner to company, use your cake decorating kit to make butter florets or use butter molds, available in gourmet shops, to mold the butters. Your dinner will look like it's been catered if you use simple, quick touches like these on your serving plates.

These sauces, butters, and marinades can also be used as a basis for your own imagination, so don't hesitate to add any ingredients you think would work.

TANGY CHERRY SAUCE
1½ cups

1 pound bing cherries, chopped coarsely
¼ cup lemon juice
1 cup water
½ cup sugar
2 tablespoons cornstarch

Combine lemon juice, water, sugar, and cornstarch in large saucepan. Stir until sugar is dissolved. Add cherries.
Micro on high 10–12 minutes until thickened. Stir once during cooking.
Note: This is great served with waterfowl.

LOW-CAL DILL SAUCE
2 cups

2 cups plain yogurt
1½ teaspoons dried dill
¼ teaspoon white pepper
½ teaspoon garlic powder
½ teaspoon oregano
Few drops Tabasco
½ teaspoon dried mustard

Combine all ingredients and chill 3–4 hours before serving with fish or vegetables or as salad dressing for a chilled salad.

ORANGE GLAZE
1¾–2 cups

    2 tablespoons cornstarch
    1 cup orange juice
    ¼ cup butter
    ⅓ cup sliced almonds
    ¼ cup dry white wine
    ¼ cup apple jelly
    ¼ cup lemon juice
    ¼ teaspoon liquid hot pepper sauce
    ⅛ teaspoon salt
    1 teaspoon orange rind, grated
    ⅔ cup canned mandarin orange sections, drained

Combine cornstarch with ¼ cup orange juice, set aside. In medium microproof saucepan, add butter and almonds and sauté 3–4 minutes on high until lightly browned. Add remaining orange juice, wine, jelly, and lemon juice; microwave on high 5 minutes. Stir in cornstarch mixture, microwave on high 5–7 minutes more, stirring once or twice, until mixture thickens. Add liquid hot pepper sauce, salt, orange rind, and orange sections. Mix well.

Cover with aluminum foil to keep warm until served. Makes about 2 cups of sauce.

BEARNAISE SAUCE

½ cup

¼ cup butter
¼ cup light cream
2 egg yolks, lightly beaten
1 tablespoon lemon juice
½ teaspoon dry mustard
¼ teaspoon salt
1 teaspoon onion, minced
1 pinch tarragon
¼ teaspoon parsley, minced
1 tablespoon vinegar

In a small, clear glass saucepan, cook butter on high 1 minute or until butter is melted. Add cream, egg yolks, lemon juice, dry mustard, and salt. Beat with mixer until smooth.

Cook on 70 percent or roast setting 1 minute, beating well with whisk every 15 seconds until thickened.

Remove from microwave and beat with electric mixer, adding remaining ingredients, until light and smooth.

Serve immediately with steaks, vegetables, or fish.

MUSTARD HOLLANDAISE SAUCE

½ cup

¼ cup butter
¼ cup light cream
2 egg yolks, well beaten
1 tablespoon lemon juice
¼ teaspoon salt, if desired
½ tablespoon powdered mustard, mixed with 1 tablespoon water

In small saucepan, cook butter on high 1 minute or until butter is melted. Add remaining ingredients.

Beat with mixer until smooth. Cook on 70 percent or roast setting 1 minute, beating well with whisk every 15 seconds until thickened.

Remove from the oven and beat with electric mixer until light and smooth. Serve with fish or vegetables.

RAISIN SAUCE

1½ cups

½ cup raisins
3 tablespoons brown sugar, packed
1 tablespoon cornstarch
1 cup apple juice
2 tablespoons lemon juice
⅛ teaspoon ground cloves
⅛ teaspoon nutmeg
⅛ teaspoon ginger

In small saucepan, mix sugar and cornstarch. Stir in apple juice and lemon juice until blended.

Cook on high 2–3 minutes, stirring every minute until thick and clear. Stir in remaining ingredients. Cook on high 1–2 minutes. Let sit 5 minutes.

Serve with waterfowl, baked squash, or baked apples.

CURRANT DUCK SAUCE

1¼ cups

¾–1 cup red currant jelly
¼ cup red wine vinegar, to taste

Mix jelly and vinegar together in glass measuring cup. Micro on high for 2 minutes. Stir well to combine.

TARTAR SAUCE

1 cup

1 cup mayonnaise
2 tablespoons sweet pickle relish
1 tablespoon lemon juice
1 tablespoon grated onion
Salt, to taste

Mix all the ingredients and refrigerate thoroughly before serving with your favorite fish dish.

Makes 1 cup of sauce.

HOT MUSTARD SAUCE

¾ cup

1 tablespoon butter
1 tablespoon flour
Salt, to taste
Freshly ground black pepper, to taste
¾ cup milk
3 tablespoons prepared mustard
1 tablespoon horseradish

Micro butter on high 1 minute. Blend in flour, salt, and pepper.

Slowly stir in milk. Micro on 50 percent for 2 minutes. Stir in mustard and horseradish. Micro on 50 percent for 1 minute. Serve warm.

MAITRE D'HOTEL BUTTER

¼ cup

4 tablespoons butter
1 teaspoon parsley, chopped finely
1 tablespoon lemon juice
Salt and pepper, to taste

Beat butter in bowl with parsley, lemon juice, salt, and pepper until light and foamy.
Note: Perfect for poached fish.

PAPRIKA BUTTER

¼ cup

4 tablespoons butter
2 teaspoons paprika

Soften 4 tablespoons butter in microwave 15 seconds on high. Add paprika. Beat with spoon until well combined.
Note: Great color addition for poached fish.

GREEN BUTTER

¼ cup

12 spinach leaves, chopped
2 tablespoons parsley, chopped
2 teaspoons fresh tarragon, chopped, or 1 teaspoon dried tarragon
4 tablespoons butter

Combine spinach, parsley, and tarragon in microproof saucepan. Add just enough water to cover. Micro on high 2 minutes. Drain dry and push through sieve or process in food processor.
Soften butter in microwave 15 seconds on high. Blend with greens and sieve again or process in food processor until smooth.
Note: Great as garnish with fish or vegetables.

CLARIFIED BUTTER

⅔ cup

1 pound butter

In small saucepan, melt butter slowly on 20 percent or low power 1½–2½ minutes, or until completely melted and oil starts to separate but has not started to simmer yet.

Remove butter from microwave and let butter sit for a few minutes. Skim off foam. Slowly pour off yellow oil and reserve.

Serve for dipping with poached or baked fish.

COOKED MARINADE

5–6 cups

1 onion, finely chopped
1 carrot, finely chopped
1 stalk celery, chopped
4 cups dry white wine
1 cup vinegar
¼ teaspoon thyme
1 tablespoon parsley, chopped
1 bay leaf, crushed
Salt, to taste
6 peppercorns, crushed

In medium microproof saucepan, combine onion, carrot, and celery. Micro on high 2 minutes.

Stir in white wine and vinegar. Add thyme and parsley, bay leaf, salt, and peppercorns. Cover lightly. Micro on high 8 minutes.

Let marinade cool, pour it over meat and let stand in refrigerator 24–36 hours, turning meat occasionally.

ALL-PURPOSE GAME MARINADE
2 cups

½ cup oil
1½ cups white vinegar
¼ teaspoon liquid smoke
1 bay leaf
½ teaspoon salt
6 tablespoons Worchestershire sauce
1 teaspoon peppercorns

Combine all ingredients. Refrigerate well before using.

Note: Good for dry cuts of game such as flank steaks, small game with little fat, or round steaks.

Convert Your Own Recipes

    Converting your favorite recipes for use in the microwave is fairly simple, especially once you have some experience cooking fish and game in your microwave oven. After you've tried some of the recipes in this book and are feeling fairly secure cooking your wild bounty, you'll probably want to convert some of your favorite recipes for use in the microwave.
    The most important change you'll need to make in your recipes is the cooking time. After you've used your microwave for a while on fish and game, you'll be able to make educated guesstimates as to the time which is most appropriate.
    In a normal oven, you can usually tell by looking at a duck, for instance, or a chukar or stuffed trout if it's properly cooked. Since your food won't have the same appearance when you pop it out of the microwave, looking at a dish is often deceiving.
    As a standard, the cooking time in a microwave is usually one-quarter the time of a conventional oven. For instance, if you normally cook a bird in your conventional oven for one hour, you'd cook the same bird in a microwave for only 15 minutes. For the recipes I convert, I usually would check it after 10 minutes and then add extra time if necessary. It's always better to undercook than to overdo it, since obviously you can add time if it's necessary.
    Yes, microwave cooking often takes some guesswork. Another thing to think about is that food continues to cook once it comes out of the microwave. In fact, some foods reach a higher temperature once they are removed from the oven.

You can capitalize on this by removing your food from the microwave just before it's completely cooked. Then cover the food with foil shiny side down, to get the best effects, for several minutes to finish the cooking.

Microwave cooking is not altogether precise. Times can't be precise due to the large number of variables that affect the results. To be a precise science or art, all the food you cook would have to be exactly the same size, shape, and weight—with the same density and the same fat and moisture content. Obviously one elk steak does not have the same exact properties as another steak, so you must be able to roll with the punches.

The amount of time needed to cook the food will also be affected by the quantity of food. In a conventional oven, it will take about an hour to cook one baked potato or five baked potatoes—the time won't change. In a microwave oven, one potato may cook in 4-6 minutes, but it may take 8-9 minutes to cook two potatoes.

When you decide to convert one of your own recipes to the microwave, look for a microwave recipe in this book, or in the cookbook that accompanied your oven, that closely matches the recipe you wish to convert. For example, look for one with the same type of main ingredients. Since most microwave cookbooks don't have many wild game or fish recipes, this cookbook should provide an excellent guide for you.

Appetizers

When converting appetizer recipes, you'll find many recipes that will work well in the microwave. Appetizers wrapped in pastry won't become crisp, though, when cooked in the microwave.

It is best to cook appetizers that contain cheese, mayonnaise, or other delicate ingredients at about 70 percent or roast setting. If you cook on high, the setting may cause separation or drying.

Heating appetizers is easy if you have a middle rack on your oven because you can double your batch. The appetizers on top will cook more quickly, though, so watch for the results.

You'll never again host a party or a wild game feed and have to worry about serving cold food—especially appetizers. It is so easy to quickly microwave your appetizers. If you must warm up your hors d'oeuvres, your guests will never know that you use the microwave to freshen them up.

Soups

When converting soup recipes for the microwave, you may have to adjust the amount of liquid you use since the brief cooking time of the microwave allows for less evaporation.

Dried bean soups won't give you good results in the microwave, so the simple solution to this problem is to use canned, precooked beans in your recipes. Don't forget to cover the dish you're using well, because the beans will often explode and make a mess of the inside of your microwave oven.

Again, when converting your recipes start with one-quarter the recommended cooking time and adjust upwards if necessary.

Meat

When choosing roasts to use in the microwave, choose evenly shaped, rolled, and tied small roasts. They'll cook better if they've been boned.

Avoid salting the surface of the meat before cooking, not only for health reasons, but because salt tends to draw liquids from the food. When cooking drier cuts of meat, especially game meat, this becomes more critical.

Game Birds

When choosing game bird recipes to use in your microwave, you'll find that most marinated recipes for birds work very nicely. You'll be surprised to find how well small birds roast though, and of course casseroles work very well in the microwave oven.

Less tender birds should be cooked on a setting no higher than 70 percent or roast, so that they don't cook too fast. It is helpful to cook on a roasting rack, if the birds are fatty as some waterfowl are.

The standing time is critical to game bird cooking. For instance, ducks or other birds cooked whole should be allowed to sit for 10–15 minutes to finish cooking. Internal temperatures will increase up to approximately 15 degrees during the standing time. Covering with foil will speed along the cooking during the standing time by reflecting and sealing in the heat.

I find the temperature probe handy when cooking fowl in the microwave. The temperature should be allowed to reach at least 170 degrees before removing from the oven. You may want to experiment with your temperature probe and your birds, though. Even though I don't like ducks cooked until they're dry (I much prefer them a little pink near the bone), I find 180 degrees is better for ducks. The best thing to do is to cook the ducks until 170 degrees and then check the birds. You can always add cooking time if necessary. In the microwave you're only talking about 5–6 minutes more probably anyway.

I would recommend trying all your converted recipes on your family and double-checking cooking times. I wouldn't serve a recipe to company the first time I converted it since sometimes the timing is uncertain. You don't want to keep your guests waiting.

Fish

To convert your recipes, begin cooking at 70 percent or roast for *one-fifth* the time recommended for the conventional oven. Then check your food and continue cooking for 30 seconds at a time. Overcooking fish in the microwave is a continual problem, so it's best to remove fish from the microwave when they're slightly undercooked and allow the standing time to finish cooking. Fish is done when it barely flakes under the fork test.

Especially since there's so much water or oil in the tissues of fish (unless they're hopelessly freezer burned), you won't need to add much liquid when you're steaming fish.

The best recipes to try in the microwave are those sautéing the fish, poaching, or casseroles. You obviously can't deep-fry fish and many coatings won't crisp in the microwave. While the microwave does have its drawbacks, you'll enjoy the fresh taste of the steamed or poached fish. When converting recipes, try those with steamed or poached fish first. You'll be hooked.

Defrosting Guide

The microwave is one of the handiest appliances in the kitchen because we all are forgetful once in a while, at least. At the last minute, when you've got nothing but frozen food to serve your family, your microwave will always bail you out. Here are some tips for defrosting fish and game in your microwave. All the suggestions here are based on using the defrosting power or 30 percent power setting of your microwave.

	Amount (pounds)	Time (minutes per pound)	Standing Time (minutes)
Ground meat	1	5–6	5
	2	8–9	5
Roast	under 5	3–5	10
	over 5	6–9	10
Round steak	1–3	4–5	5–10
Steak	2–3	4–5	5–10
Chops	3–4	5–8	15
Sausage	1	2–3	3–5
Stew meat	2	4–5	8–10
Duck	3–5	4–5	30–40
Goose	8–10	3–5	40–60
Quail, dove, woodcock	1–3	2–3	40–60
Chukar, grouse	3–5	3–5	40–60
Pheasant	5–8	5–8	40–60
Rabbit	3–5	5–8	40–60
Squirrel	3–5	5–8	40–60
Fish fillet	1 or under	4–6	5
	over 1	5–7	5
Fish steak	1 or under	4–6	5
	2	5–7	5
Whole fish	1 or under	4–6	5
	over 1	5–7	5

Tips

- Turn packages over once during cooking time.
- Freeze ground meat in shape of doughnut to facilitate thawing.
- Remove the defrosted ground meat from edges halfway through defrosting time.
- Separate chops, stew meat, and steaks as they're thawed enough.
- Defrost packages on a plate to hold drippings.
- Separate whole birds when partially thawed.
- Immerse birds in cold water for standing time, if desired, to speed defrosting.
- Cover wing tips and leg tips with aluminum foil as soon as they appear thawed to prevent cooking.
- Separate fish fillets and steaks under cold water.
- Whole fish should be icy when removed from oven.
- Cover the heads and tails of whole fish with aluminum foil to protect them from cooking.

Index

Alagnak River, 119, 168
Alaska, 119–120, 126, 168
Antelope, 76–82
Antelope, recipes
    Antelope Chops, 76
    Antelope Kabobs, 78
    Fast Antelope Steaks, 80–81
    Garden Fresh Gumbo, 79
    Jay Dahl's Curried Antelope, 81
    Saucy Barbecued Chops, 80
    Sausage Canapes, 151
    Stuffed Antelope Chops, 82
Appetizers, 146–147
Appetizers, recipes
    Antelope Sausage Canapes, 151
    Artichoke Hearts, 154
    Cheese and Fish Dip, 153
    Creamy Salmon Dip, 149
    Hot Fish Canapes, 151
    Hot Salmon Dip, 150
    Joe Green's Chukar Bits, 148
    Marinated Mushrooms, 148
    Sausage Balls, 150
    Swedish Meatballs, 152–153

Bass, 103–105
Bass, recipes
    Bayou Bass, 106
    Creamy Bass, 108
    Glazed Bass Fillets, 106–107
    Italian Bass Fillets, 105
    Pesce Con Pesto, 107
    Striped Bass Rolls, 108
Breads, 165–166
    Mexican Cornbread, 165
    Sourdough Blueberry Muffins, 166
    Orange Pecan Muffins, 166
Butters, recipes
    Clarified Butter, 178
    Green Butter, 177
    Maitre D'Hotel Butter, 177
    Paprika Butter, 177

California, 138, 143
Caribou, Moose and, 99
Caribou, recipe
    German-Style Caribou Pot Roast, 100

Catfish, 109
Catfish, recipes
    Catfish Fillets, 113
    Catfish in Horseradish Sauce, 112
    Catfish with Mushrooms and
        Buttermilk, 111
    Garlic Catfish, 110
Chilton, Kathy, 161
Chukar, 17-18
Chukar, recipes
    Chukar Au Vin, 21
    Chukar Tetrazzini, 22
    Dr. Tom's 40 Garlic Chukar, 20
    Grilled Chukar, 19
    Orange Glazed Chukars, 22
Convert Your Own Recipes
    Appetizers, 181
    Fish, 183
    Game Birds, 182-183
    Meat, 182
    Soups, 182

Deer, 82-84
Deer, recipes
    Burgundy Venison Stew, 90
    Easy Venison Ragout, 89
    Kielbasa Sandwiches, 87
    Pepper Steak, 86
    Taco Salad, 86-87
    Terrific Teriyaki, 85
    Venison Peppers, 84
    Venison Skillet Dinner, 87
    Venison Stew, 88
Defrosting Guide, 184-185
Desserts, recipes
    Amaretto Strawberries and Ice Cream, 168
    Baked Apples, 169
    Blackberry Sourdough Cobbler, 169
    The Braids Chocolate Bananas, 168
Dove, 23-24
Dove, recipes
    Creamy Mushroom Doves, 24-25
    Doves Ole!, 25
    Peachy Doves, 26-27
    Savory Doves, 27
    Southern Style Doves, 26
    Soy Sauced Doves, 28
    Spicy Doves, 28-29
Duck, 44-46

Duck, recipes
    Barbecued Duck Breasts, 50
    Cherry Sauced Duck Breasts, 46
    Ducks in Apple and Cream Sauce, 48-49
    Ducks with Bacon and Onions, 46-47
    Ducks with Sauerkraut and Apples, 49
    Easy Duck Soup, 48
    Spinach Casseroled Duck Breasts, 47

Elk, 90-92
Elk, recipes
    Elk Chilironi, 94-95
    Elk Sirloin Steaks, 94
    Elk Steak Pizzaiola, 96-97
    Fantastic Elk Stroganoff, 93
    Hawaiian-Style Elk Chops, 98
    Marinated Elk Steaks, 96
    Savory Elk Roast, 95
    Swiss Chops, 97
    Three-Bean Elk Chili, 92
Elko, Nevada, 17, 103

Flounder, 138-139
Flounder, recipes
    Lemon Flounder, 139
    Stuffed Flounder, 140

Gallagher, Tom and Dorothy, 11, 20, 162
Goose, 51-52
Goose, recipes
    Goose Stuffed with Raisins and Orange
        Sauce, 54
    Goose with Apricot and Prune Stuffing, 53
    Wild Rice and Sausage Stuffed Goose, 55
Ground Hog, recipe
    Burgundy Cream Ground Hog, 70
Grouse, 29-30
Grouse, recipes, 30-32
    Curried Sage Grouse Salad, 31
    Grouse Au Vin, 32
    Orange Stuffed Grouse, 30-31

Halibut, 140-141

Halibut, recipes
    Halibut Almondine, 142
    Halibut in Cheese Sauce, 141
    Halibut Steaks with Sesame Seeds, 142–143
Hors d'oeuvres, 28, 148–154. *See also* Appetizers

Jacksnipe, 41–43

Lake Mead, 104
Lake Tahoe, 126
Las Vegas News Bureau, 104
Leftovers, recipes
    Chukar Tetrazzini, 22–23
    Curried Sage Grouse Salad, 31
    Pesce Con Pesto, 107

Marinades, recipes
    Cooked Marinade, 178
    All-Purpose Game Marinade, 179
Mixed Bag, 68–69
Mixed Bag, recipes
    Baked Wild Boar Chops, 72–73
    Burgundy Cream Ground Hog, 70
    Leg of Wild Boar, 73
    Peppery Raccoon, 72
    Stewed Up Raccoon, 71
Moose and Caribou, 99
Moose, recipes
    Moose Sauerbraten, 101
    Roast Moose with Vegetables, 102
Muffins, recipes
    Orange Pecan Muffins, 166–167
    Sourdough Blueberry Muffins, 166

Nevada, 17, 23, 29–30, 32–33, 52, 103–104, 119, 126, 132, 134, 138
Nevada Department of Wildlife, 58
New York, 139

Panfish, 113–114
Panfish, recipes

Brochettes of Bluegill, 118
Fish Rolls, 116
Gingered Panfish Fillets, 114–115
Panfish Alberti, 117
Panfish Casserole, 116–117
Panfish Parmigiana, 115
Pheasant, 32–33
Pheasant, recipes
    Cheesy Cheddar Pheasant, 34
    Creamy Pheasant, 36
    Pheasant and Mushrooms, 36–37
    Roast Pheasant, 35
    Souped Up Pheasant, 34–35
Pike, Walleye and, 134
Pike, recipes
    Herbed Pike, 137
    Pike with Creamed Shrimp Sauce, 135
Potatoes, recipes
    Sour Cream Potato Casserole, 163
    Parsley New Potatoes, 164
Pyramid Lake, Nevada, 126

Quail, 37–38
Quail, recipes
    Quail in Mushrooms, 40–41
    Quail in Parmesan Sauce, 39
    Quail Marsala, 40
    Quail with Grapes, 38

Rabbit, 57–58
Rabbit, recipes
    Hasenpfeffer, 59
    Mexican Rabbit, 64
    Rabbit Cacciatore, 62
    Rabbit Cacciatore Too, 63
    Rabbit in White Wine, 60
    Rabbit with Curry Sauce, 61
Raccoon, recipes
    Peppery Raccoon, 72
    Stewed Up Raccoon, 71
Reno, Nevada, 119, 138

Salad, recipes
    Aunt Rose and Nettie's Olive and Celery Salad, 157

Caraway Slaw, 159
Curried Sage Grouse Salad, 31
Herbed Trout and Macaroni Salad, 130
Hot Spinach Salad, 158
Marinated Cucumber Salad, 157
Sauerkraut Salad, 158
Taco Salad, 86
Salmon, 118–120
Salmon, recipes
    Baked Salmon, 124
    Fettucine Al Salmon, 121
    Florentine Salmon, 124–125
    Garlic Salmon, 122
    Poached Salmon Steaks, 121
    Quick Salmon Casserole, 122
    Salmon Quiche, 120
    Stuffed Salmon Steaks, 123
Sauces, recipes
    Bearnaise Sauce, 174
    Currant Duck Sauce, 175
    Hot Mustard Sauce, 176
    Lo-Cal Dill Sauce, 172
    Mustard Hollandaise Sauce, 174
    Orange Glaze, 173
    Raisin Sauce, 175
    Tangy Cherry Sauce, 172
    Tartar Sauce, 176
Serve Alongs, 155–156
Serve Alongs, recipes
    Amaretto Strawberries and Ice Cream, 168
    Asparagus Vinaigrette, 159
    Aunt Rose and Nettie's Olive and Celery Salad, 157
    Baked Apples, 169
    Blackberry Sourdough Cobbler, 167
    Butternutty Squash, 161
    Caraway Slaw, 159
    Dorothy's Cabbage Casserole, 162
    Glazed Carrots and Peas, 160
    Hot Salsa, 162
    Hot Spinach Salad, 158
    Kathy Chilton's Mexican Bean Dip, 161
    Marinated Cucumber Salad, 157
    Mexican Cornbread, 165
    Nutty Wild Rice, 164
    Orange Pecan Muffins, 166–167
    Parsley New Potatoes, 164
    Sauerkraut Salad, 158
    Sour Cream Potato Casserole, 163
    Sourdough Blueberry Muffins, 166
    The Braids Chocolate Bananas, 168

Sierra Mountains, 126
Soups, recipes
    Easy Duck Soup, 48
    Garden Fresh Gumbo, 79
    Three-Bean Elk Chili, 92
Sourdough, recipes
    Blackberry Sourdough Cobbler, 167
    Sourdough Blueberry Muffins, 166
Squirrel, 65
Squirrel, recipes
    Breaded Baked Squirrel, 66
    Squash and Squirrel, 67
Stew, recipes
    Burgundy Venison Stew, 90
    Venison Stew, 88
Stuffing, recipes
    Apple Stuffing, 56
    Apricot and Prune Stuffing, 53
    Raisin Stuffing, 54
    Wild Rice and Sausage Stuffing, 55
Sturgeon, 143
Sturgeon, recipes
    Market Street Sturgeon Steaks, 144
    Spicy Tomato Sturgeon, 145

Trout, 125–126
Trout, recipes
    Baked Orange Trout, 133
    Bernardied Brookies, 132–133
    Crab Stuffed Trout, 129
    Herbed Trout and Macaroni Salad, 130
    Mushroom Stuffed Trout, 128
    Scuffy's Camp Brookies, 132
    Tarragon Trout, 127
    Wildhorse Ratatouille Trout, 131

Vegetables, recipes
    Asparagus Vinaigrette, 159
    Butternutty Squash, 161
    Dorothy's Cabbage Casserole, 162
    Glazed Carrots and Peas, 160
    Magic Corn On The Cob, 160
    Parsley New Potatoes, 164
    Sour Cream Potato Casserole, 163

Walleye and Pike, 134
Walleye, recipes

Spicy Walleye, 136
Walleye Provencal, 136
Wild Boar, recipes
    Baked Wild Boar Chops, 72–73
    Leg of Wild Boar, 73

Wildhorse, 131
Woodcock, 41–42
Woodcock, recipes
    Brandied Woodcock, 42
    Woodcock in Wine Sauce, 43